Iredell County

NORTH CAROLINA

Iredell County

NORTH CAROLINA

A BRIEF HISTORY

Sandra Douglas Campbell

Charleston | London
THE
History
PRESS

Published by The History Press
Charleston, SC 29403
www.historypress.net

Cover image: The Old Courthouse (circa 1899), Iredell County Seat, Statesville, North Carolina. *Original watercolor courtesy of Michael Joe Moore.*

First published 2008

Manufactured in the United Kingdom

ISBN 978.1.59629.338.0

Library of Congress Cataloging-in-Publication Data

Campbell, Sandra Douglas.
Iredell County, North Carolina : a brief history / Sandra Douglas Campbell.
p. cm.
ISBN 978-1-59629-338-0
1. Iredell County (N.C.)--History. I. Title.
F262.I7C36 2008
975.6'793--dc22
                                        2008019188

To Theresa Golas, Director of Iredell Museums, which is the repository of so very many legacies from Iredell County residents; and to all of the tireless historians and historic preservation organizations that help us remember "who we are."

Contents

Preface

Thomas Wolfe said that we are the sum of the moments in our lives, but we are so much more. We are the sum of all those who have gone before us, and their legacies inform us and shape our lives. This brief history of Iredell County provides a look at our county and its towns and villages at various moments in time, from the county's beginnings to the twenty-first century. It also documents the places and the things that we, individually and collectively, are preserving for future generations. We are fortunate that our Southern traditions embrace the past and create continuity from generation to generation. We know that we are the caretakers of the legacies of our forebears. We know that history is all around us. Enjoy this little walk through history—it will only take a moment of your time—and you will marvel at how far we have come and how much of our past has been preserved. Kenneth Clarke wrote that we need to know that we belong somewhere in time, and we need to be able to look both forward and back. History gives us access to this "looking back" through the places and things that we preserve. This is now our legacy to the future. It is a gift, and a gift that only we can give.

Acknowledgements

Ms. Theresa Golas, Director, Iredell Museums and the Board of Directors

Mr. O.C. Stonestreet, Educator, Historian and Columnist, Statesville *Record and Landmark*

Mr. Paul Brendle and Mr. Jim Sutton, Private Collectors

Dr. Steve Hill, Collector and Vice-President of Education, Iredell/Statesville Schools

Ms. Mickey Vacca, Archaeologist and Educator

Mr. H. Andy Poore, Local History Department, Mooresville Public Library

Mr. Dennis Goodin and Mrs. Selena Goodin, the Historic Vance House and Civil War Museum

Ms. Beth Hill, Manager, Fort Dobbs State Historic Site

Mr. Lewis Alexander, Private Collector and Restoration Specialist

Mr. Joel Reese, Local History Librarian, Iredell County Library

Mr. John Steele, President, J.C. Steele and Sons

Mrs. Ralph Bentley, Mrs. Edwin Hunter and the Sharpe House Board of Trustees

Mr. Gene Krider, Architect and Author

Mr. David Bradley, President, Greater Statesville Chamber of Commerce

Mr. Jim King, Town Planner, Mooresville

Mr. Wayne Frick, Mooresville Downtown Commission

Mr. Richard Boyd, Statesville Historic Properties Commission

Ms. Cynthia Jacobs, Mooresville Historical Society

Chapter 1

1700–1776

The Land Before European Settlement and Our Pioneer American Forefathers

The Piedmont

We passed through a delicious country, none that I ever saw exceeds it. We saw fine bladed grass six feet high along the banks of these pleasant rivulets. Coming about thirty miles we reached the fertile and pleasant banks of the Sapona (Yadkin) River whereon stands the Indian town and fort…a pleasant savannah land with heavily wooded ridges and creek banks.

—*John Lawson, eighteenth-century explorer*

The name "Piedmont" means "foot of the mountains," and originally referred to an area of Italy—*piemonte*—at the foot of the Alps. The land that would become Iredell County is at the western edge of the Piedmont physiographic area, a 125-mile-wide region of irregular, hilly land. Predominately ridges, with valleys scored by streams feeding two major rivers (the Yadkin and the Catawba), north Iredell presents a gently rolling landscape. The soft foothills of the Blue Ridge, the Brushy Mountains, erupt in the far northern corner of the county. Fox Mountain, elevation 1,760 feet, is the highest point. South Iredell is more typically Piedmont with flat uplands interrupted by streams.

A number of creeks flow across Iredell, their creek bottoms crowded with river cane, a bamboo-like species native to the Southeast. At one time, wild pea vines covered the hills and meadows. Eighty species of trees are native to Iredell, including ten species of oak, five of hickory, two of pine and five of magnolia. Today our creeks, fords and some of our roads are still called by names that would have been familiar to the eighteenth-century pioneers who settled this area.

Collier Cobb, of the University of North Carolina–Chapel Hill, coined the phrase "nature's sample case" to encapsulate the huge variety of plants and minerals in the area. For further reading on the natural history of this area, see: *Heritage of Iredell County*, Vol. I, published by the Genealogical Society of Iredell County, which contains an excellent article by Louis Brown; and *Iredell, Piedmont County*, written by Homer Keever, which offers exceptional detail of our "nature's sample case." Iredell Museums in Statesville houses an extensive collection of minerals from the area and has connections to the Statesville Greenway Project including a bog walk and trails at Gregory Creek and Indian Ridge.

The foothills of the Brushy Mountains stand as sentinels in the far northwestern corner of Iredell County, accenting the rare rural beauty even in the twenty-first century. Fortunately, the railroads did not reach this pastoral area, leaving it to its agrarian roots and preserving an irreplaceable natural landscape. *Photograph by Max Tharpe. Courtesy of Mitchell Community College.*

A 1996 inventory by Christopher Frye identified twenty-six significant Natural Heritage Areas in Iredell County. In 2005, there were twenty-two, with one of national importance and two of state significance. The North Carolina Natural Heritage Program can be accessed at www.ncnhp.org. The Land Trust for Central North Carolina works toward preserving our rural landscape and natural heritage by designating acreage to be protected from development and preserved as farmland, woodland or open areas for the future benefit of every citizen. Information on the organization can be accessed at www. openspaceprotection.org and at the following address: landtrust@landtrustnc.org. Their mission is "to work thoughtfully and selectively with property owners to preserve our lands, our vistas, and the essential nature of our region" and honoring their dedication to conservation will ultimately save the legacy of the natural areas in Iredell.

Native Americans

As a race they have withered from the land…they are shrinking before the mighty tide which is pressing them away. They must soon hear the roar of the last wave which will settle over them forever.
—Sam Houston

The Piedmont was an Indian hunting ground, shared by the Catawbas and the Cherokees. Other smaller tribes peopled the area: Sapona, Saura, Sugaree and Waxhaw; however, they eventually were absorbed by the Catawba people, whose nation was a military alliance of several Siouan tribes. Archaeological evidence of their lives is abundant and includes arrowheads, clay pipes, vessels, shells, gourds, beads, hooks, needles, mortars, anvils, scrapers, axes, drills, pendants, hoes and spades. Local historian Homer Keever maintained that a site on Third Creek could contain artifacts dating from 2000 BC, left by native people predating the Catawbas, who were an established tribe well before the early explorers arrived at the end of the seventeenth century. Another site is east of Fourth Creek, and it is referenced in a 1751 land grant as having a campsite and buffalo licks on the creek.

Howard Zinn wrote in *The People's History of the United States* that the explorers, traders, surveyors and pioneers were "not coming into an empty wilderness, but into a world which in some places was as densely populated as Europe itself." They came into a world where "the culture was complex; where human relations were more egalitarian than in Europe; and where the relations among men, women, children, and nature were more beautifully worked out than perhaps any place in the world." The Indian was a part of the "natural world" in ways we cannot understand. Joseph Campbell, writing in *The Power of Myth*, describes a powerful, magical world that was, and is now, beyond European understanding. Into this magical world, that was both "sophisticated and natural," came the Europeans. Beginning with a few intrepid explorers and surveyors, the flood of immigrants thereafter did not cease.

John Lederer, known as the "Father of Explorers in the Piedmont," traveled the Yadkin River Valley in 1670. John Lawson, an English surveyor, passed through Iredell about the year 1700 on his trip from Charles Towne (Charleston) to the eastern part of North Carolina. He noted that most early explorers were "persons of the meaner sort and generally of very slender education." They traded coarse cloth and edged tools for a huge variety of fur (deer hide in North Carolina) and realized enormous profits. Both Lawson and Lederer left descriptions of the Catawba Indians, calling them "handsome, with a very straight carriage, having a civil nature and a sedate, majestic gait." The Catawbas were of the Sioux Nation and were a well-settled agricultural people, skillful as potters and weavers. In *The American Indian in North Carolina*, Douglas Rights recounts his experience with the Catawba people who still make pottery in the traditional manner of hand building, even though many contemporary Catawbas have not seen the work of their ancestors. Rights took a small group of Catawbas to a museum and there they saw the work of their forebears for the first time.

The Catawbas taught the pioneers woodcraft and agriculture, introducing corn, potatoes and tobacco. The traditional Indian planting design, "The Three Sisters," was another gift to the settlers—corn, beans and squash are all planted in the same hill, thus the rather elegant planting scheme. Jack Weatherford writes in *Native Roots* that there were approximately eighty food and medicinal plants that the Indians shared with the pioneer newcomers and that "the great majority of crops exhibited at county fairs came from Indian agriculture." Weatherford adds, "In all the years since, no one has found a single plant suitable for domestication that Indians had not already cultivated." Tobacco was a New World crop that was introduced to Europe by the Spanish about 1585, but it was common to the Indians, who smoked the dried leaves ceremonially. It had spread from Mexico, along with sunflowers, centuries before European contact with the New World, which is generally dated 1524–1662 and called the "Period of Discovery and Exploration."

Sharing this Piedmont area with the Catawbas were the Cherokees, a rugged Iroquois people who controlled the mountainous area that spread over six Southeastern states. Latecomers to the Piedmont, they shared the Catawba hunting ground that was to become Iredell County. Hereditary enemies of the Catawbas, the Cherokees were hunters, sportsmen and gamblers, with an unfortunate vengeful streak. Their ballgames were called "the little wars" and their war games favored surprise attacks in the early hours of the morning. They can, however, be credited with teaching the settlers the tactics of guerilla warfare, enabling the colonists to later defeat the premier empire of the time, the British Empire.

Henry Timberlake, a British army officer, described the Cherokees as "well featured, straight and well built of middle stature." They had a penchant for jewelry and piercing, would cover their skin with tattoos tinted with gunpowder (guns were introduced circa 1700) and would pluck out or shave almost all the hair on their heads. Charles Royce and James Mooney, leading authorities on the Cherokees of the late nineteenth and early twentieth centuries, wrote: "The Cherokee are probably the largest and most important tribe in the United States, having their own national government; abundant records, concluding more treaties with the government than any other tribe; and their own invented alphabet, effectively preserving their spoken language." The Cherokees

Catawba beaded gourd. *Courtesy of Iredell Museums.*

were driven to a far corner of North Carolina by the end of 1836, when they finally surrendered the last tribal land to the government with the Treaty of New Echota. Much too soon, they were once again forced to resettle in Oklahoma on reservations, although many hid in the mountains of North Carolina, refusing to leave their ancestral homeland.

A local American Indian collection is a private collection formerly belonging to Mr. Paul Brendle and is now the collection of Mr. Jim Sutton, who has acquired almost half of Brendle's enormous collection of thousands of artifacts. Mr. Sutton's collection includes one large clay pot found at Third Creek, which, though structurally damaged, is a stellar example of tribal decorative arts. (Brendle was featured in the *Iredell Citizen* on April 7, 2005. Mr. Sutton acquired one half of the collection in 2006.)

Most of the collection was found in an area bounded by the foothills, the lower Pee Dee Valley, the Yadkin River, and the Catawba River. Mr. Brendle, who had been collecting since the 1940s, recommends Frank K. Barnard for further reading on artifacts; the 1876 classic, *North American Indians*, by George Catlin, is also an outstanding resource. A remarkable number of items were found in 1991 and 1992 at Hunting Creek. Another rare find is a group of clear quartz arrow points, ten thousand years old, found in the Harmony area.

Iredell Museums has an extensive collection from the area in its Native American collection. A seed pot from the Pee Dee Period, circa AD 1500, is an extraordinary

Rare fifteenth-century seed pot from the Pee Dee excavation. *Courtesy of Iredell Museums.*

discovery and one of only a few examples in the Southeastern United States. The upper Pee Dee is the Yadkin River, and there the seed pot was found in a burial site. Artifacts have also been found near Lake Norman and in Union Grove in an area near Jennings Mill known as Indian Hill. Many relics were unearthed in the northeast corner of Mooresville during the building of the town. This area was bounded by three streams, forming a lake and creating a shallow, watery bog. Stone fire pits were left by Indians as well as stones for weighting fishing nets, rubbing and skinning stones, pottery shards and flints. Slick Rock Park in Mooresville was once considered a site of sacred water and flints can still be found there. (There are two large private collections of artifacts in Mooresville as well.)

P.F. Laugenour, noted local historian in the early twentieth century, related the story of a flood in 1901 near Statesville, which exposed an Indian graveyard at the lower end of Long Island "on the edge of the old Kestler Plantation." Laugenour stated that the site was not preserved, even though jewelry, pottery and remains were uncovered by floodwaters. It is our loss. The artifacts would have revealed a priceless history of an ancient people now untraceable, now vanished from the land. Today, archaeological discoveries remain in danger of being lost to encroaching development.

The Pioneers

They were a motley group, those white Americans. Composed of English, Scot, Irish, French, Dutch, Germans, and Swedes…melted into a new race of men whose labors and posterity caused great changes in the world.

—St. John de Crevecoeur

The proprietary era is generally dated from 1663 to 1729, so called because King Charles II granted what is now both Carolinas to eight nobles, the Lord Proprietors. They were granted enormous tracts for the pivotal role they played in returning Charles II to the throne, thus restoring the monarchy in England. By 1710, all territory from southern Virginia to the coast of Florida was granted, including all natural resources, discovered or not. The proprietors were also given broad powers with the authority to create governing officers, establish courts, assess penalties and levy taxes. In return, the colonists were to be awarded the same rights as Englishmen. North Carolina began to grow, albeit slowly, in the 1720s. The king again took control in 1729 and all of the Lord Proprietors sold their rights back to the crown with the exception of Lord Carteret. John, Baron Carteret, Earl of Granville, would continue to grant land and collect rents until his death.

The war with the Tuscaroras (1711-1713) on the coastal plain resulted in the opening of the Piedmont to settlement. It is considered a turning point in the development of the western part of the state. The overcrowded coastal colonies began to lose settlers who were pushing west for the ever more valuable land. Additionally, to the north, Pennsylvania began to lose settlers. Land had become expensive, if available at all, and because of the French and Indian War the area was seen as increasingly dangerous. In the future south Iredell, over half of the land was open, with some fields already cultivated by the Catawbas. Former coastal settlers and second-generation German (Pennsylvania Dutch) and Scottish settlers from Pennsylvania, and those from Virginia and Maryland as well, poured into this open land between 1738 and 1776.

Foote, in *Sketches of North Carolina*, wrote, "Scattered settlements of white people were made along the Catawba River from Beatty's Ford to Mason's Ford sometime before the county became the object of emigration to any great extent, probably around 1740." There were settlers between the Yadkin and Catawba Rivers and along Fourth Creek by 1746, and by 1749 settlers were well established in the south of the future county. In February of 1750, Granville's agents conducted a survey along Fourth Creek for the Oliphant family. The Oliphant's 640 acres included the area upon which Statesville would eventually be built and was centrally located in the Fourth Creek area. For details on the Granville grants, see W.N. Watt, writing for the Genealogical Society of Iredell County, in the *Heritage of Iredell County*; Homer Keever's detailed history, *Iredell, Piedmont County*; and the Archives of the North Carolina State Library in Raleigh.

Life in the eighteenth century was fraught with danger from a wild, unfamiliar country and frontier life, as well as from common practices of the time. Medicine was still stifled by the medieval belief in the four humors in the body that controlled its vitality and fitness; bloodletting and purging were the preferred methods used to "restore good

Eighteenth-century cradle with Scots-Irish heart design. *Courtesy of Iredell Museums.*

health." Anesthesia was not yet developed; babies born had only a 50 percent chance of surviving into adulthood; privacy was nonexistent in homes as well as public inns; candles and firelight provided illumination after sunset and fire was the only source of heat; and sanitary facilities included pots, buckets and outhouses. Ordinary people lived in a plain and frugal manner and battled then common diseases such as dysentery, pleurisy, fever and ague (tremors or shaking). Meals, prepared on the open fire, were taken on wooden trenchers with "noggins" holding a pint of liquid used for drink. Coffee was rarely used except for the sick. Clothing was made of tow (combed and carded flax) or cotton and coats were made of a mix of cotton and wool; aprons were stitched from homemade linen, bleached white and saved for Sunday. Almost all settlers were farmers except for the few town dwellers in every village. Slavery was legal in all the colonies and women, having no rights, were not even allowed to own property, unless widowed.

Travel was torturously slow and difficult, covering only twenty or thirty miles a day, and following the few trodden paths already existing "in the wild." These paths were Indian trails, or traces, usually running along creek banks, ridges and buffalo paths. The buffalo in the area made trails across the mountains and close grazed the land, even down to the early-growth small evergreens. (It is speculated that this close grazing kept the county an open plain, with few naturally reforested areas.) One of the most well-documented and

Blanket chest circa 1750–1790, with original locks and hinges. *Courtesy of Iredell Museums.*

well-used early trails is Sherrill's Path, which traced a route from Sherrill's Ford on the Catawba to Shallow Ford on the Yadkin. A detailed description of Sherrill's Path and its likely route is contained in two articles by W.N. Watt in *Heritage of Iredell County*. The path was named for the Sherrill family, one of the earliest arrivals who came south via the Trading Path, another well-known Indian trace. The Trading Path was sometimes called the Great South Road, traversing the southern end of the county to a ford on the Catawba, later settled by the Beatty family and ever after known as Beatty's Ford. The path passed through Iredell north of Mooresville and Mount Mourne. P.F. Laugenour credited the early settlement of the Centre congregation to its proximity to this path. Fourth Creek, Statesville's premier settlement, is close to the path as well.

Another Indian warrior's path would become known as the Great Philadelphia Wagon Road, although any semblance of a roadway, or even a farm track, would tax the imagination. The English gained usage of this route by treaty with the Iroquois. The trail began at the Iroquois Confederacy on the Great Lakes and culminated at Salem and Salisbury where it joined the Catawba–Cherokee Trading Path, which itself crossed the Yadkin River at Shallow Ford. It was sometimes called the Carolina Road but most often it was called the Great Wagon Road and it was used by settlers arriving in the future Iredell County. R.W. Ramsey traced movement on the Great Wagon Road in

Carolina Cradle. In 1752 alone, over four hundred families migrated south using this route where the rivers had acceptable fords and the hills were modest and could be managed by wagons. It was a seven-hundred-mile length of rough travel; however, by the year 1765, it was clear enough for horse-drawn wagons and the population between the rivers grew apace. Carl Bridenbaugh wrote, "In the last sixteen years of the Colonial Period southbound traffic along the Great Wagon Road was numbered in tens of thousands. It was the most heavily traveled road in America."

Bishop Spangenberg's survey in 1752 stated, "Hitherto we have been on a trading path where we could find at least one house a day where food could be bought; but from here we turn into pathless forest." He was, at the time, west of the future site of Statesville, on the Catawba River, and although he called it "pathless," the forest was clear of underbrush because of large burned areas cleared by the Indians to facilitate their hunting. Spangenberg also wrote, "Having crossed the length and breadth of North Carolina, we have found that toward the west nearer the mountains, many families are moving in from Virginia, Maryland, Pennsylvania and Jersey, and even New England. This year alone more than four hundred families have come with horse and wagon, and cattle. Among them are sturdy farmers and skilled men." Bishop Spangenberg's "Moravian Diary" can be accessed in *Colonial Records*, Vol. IV, p. 312, and Vol. V, pp. 1–4, and online at www.ah.dcr.state.nc.us/sections/hp/colonial/bookshelf.Moravian/diary.htm.

Rowan County was formed in 1753, but well before it was established, pioneers were settling the upper ends of Third, Fourth and Fifth Creeks, all so named because they are the third, fourth and fifth creeks crossed as one travels from Salisbury toward Statesville. Almost all of the settlers were Scots-Irish, often called Ulster-Scots. They were so named because they were Scots who had taken advantage of the English Plantation System developed in Northern Ireland as a vehicle to resettle the Ulster area with English sympathizers. This system originated with King James (VI of Scotland, I of England) about 1604, after the conspiracy of the Irish Earls of Tyrconnell and Tyrone, whose extensive holdings then escheated to the crown. The king awarded the confiscated estates to any Scots who would settle there. The antagonism between the Catholic Irish and the Protestant Scots prevented intermarriage. Ulster-Scot, or Scots-Irish, is basically a geographical description, not a statement of ethnicity, only used in the United States and primarily by genealogists.

Our church records and cemeteries are often the only remnants of this first generation of settlers. Fortunately, there were many churches established by those pioneers, initially adhering to the state church of Scotland, the Presbyterian Church. There were preaching stands at various locations where services were held but few churches had yet been organized. These stands were merely rock outcroppings or rough platforms built between two trees. An early "preaching stand" is on Chipley Ford Road at Museum Road in Statesville. In the year 1753, it was used by the Fourth Creek Presbyterian congregation until the Meeting House could be built in the mid-1750s in Statesville.

Coddle Creek Church, five miles east of Mooresville, is the Associate Reformed Presbyterians' oldest church, established in 1753. It is the oldest ARP church in North

Eighteenth-century handmade corner
cupboard with Moravian-style rattail
hinges. *Courtesy of Iredell Museums.*

Carolina and the second oldest in the United States. The burying ground behind
the church was established that same year and its oldest headstone is dated 1757. A
1755 diary entry refers to the Coddle Creek Meeting House as a log structure. This
log building lasted until 1839, when it was replaced by a second building that was
destroyed by a fire that also consumed its early records in 1884. The third church
building was erected that same year and is the present church building which sits on
a wide green lawn in the countryside, its original state altered only by the addition of
siding in 1988.

The early settlers of Davidson Creek are buried at Centre Presbyterian Church,
which first met at Osborne's Meeting House northeast of Davidson College. Centre was
established in 1765 at Mount Mourne, near Mooresville. Their first building burned in
1775. The present church was built in 1854. Made of handmade bricks, it is styled in
the classic temple form of Greek Revival design, with its interior intact including the
gaslight fixtures, which were altered much later for the use of electricity. Centre is on
the National Register of Historic Places and is maintained as it was originally built and
furnished, although all records pre-1839 are lost.

Coddle Creek ARP Church, established in 1753, now occupies a country Victorian building erected in 1884. *Courtesy of the author.*

Centre Presbyterian Church, established 1765, now occupies a Greek Revival building built with handmade bricks in 1854. *Courtesy of the author.*

In 1773, William Sharpe produced a map justifying a desire to split the Fourth Creek congregation into thirds—Fourth Creek, now First Presbyterian, remained in the Meeting House. By 1758, the adjacent Fourth Creek Burying Ground had been established as well. (The term "meetinghouse" was not used after the Revolution and the word "congregation" supplanted the quaint term.) Morrison's congregation was the second to be formed in 1775 and is now Concord Presbyterian Church. Their group worship began at a preaching stand at Morrison's Mill around 1750. The small Morrison Cemetery, one mile southwest of Loray near Concord Presbyterian Church, was used by Concord Church before 1822; after that date, the cemetery behind the church was used. The present church building is the fourth, circa 1939. The third congregation formed at Bethany Church, established circa 1773–1775. The present church was built around 1855. The cemetery, dating from 1785, includes the graves of pioneers and Revolutionary War soldiers enclosed in a picturesque dry-stone wall. The site of the home and academy of Dr. James Hall was near the church.

The first Baptist church, Grassy Knob, was established circa 1788–1789, and it is the oldest Baptist congregation in Iredell. It is located at the foot of a small mountain called Grassy Knob near the Wilkes County line. The present building dates from 1953, but the cemetery's oldest inscription is 1801.

Mount Bethel is the oldest Methodist congregation, established in 1797 at Basil Prather's home, called Prather's Meeting House. Snow Creek Methodist began as a

Bethany Presbyterian Church, established circa 1773–1775, now occupies a simple building erected in 1855. *Courtesy of the author.*

Methodist Society and is another of Iredell's older Methodist congregations, with a cemetery at Snow Creek established by 1780. In 1801, King's Methodist Episcopal Church was built beside the cemetery. The name was later changed to Snow Creek and the new church, a Late Greek Revival frame building, was built in 1881. The old cemetery has one hundred antebellum markers dating from 1817 on the grounds of the church, which is little changed. McKendree Chapel first met as Mayhew's Meeting House in 1793. The building burned in 1804, but was rebuilt that same year and renamed McKendree Chapel Methodist Episcopal Church. The cemetery is one of the older ones in Iredell.

Some of the oldest cemeteries in Iredell County include: St. Michael's Lutheran Church Cemetery and St. Martin's Community Cemetery near Troutman; Sharon Lutheran Church Cemetery, circa 1849; New Sterling Church Cemetery, circa 1802; the Troutman Family Cemetery; Sharpe's Burying Ground at Yadkin Baptist Church; the Scroggs Cemetery in the Barium Springs area; the Lewis Family Burying Ground; the Campbell Family Cemetery in Union Grove; the Young Family Cemetery in Houstonville (oldest marker: 1797); and the Allison Graveyard, circa 1758, in Statesville. P.F. Laugenour, writing for the *Sentinel* in 1916, stated: "While the graveyard at Centre has some claims to antiquity, and Fourth Creek dates back to 1760-1765, and Morrison's is not of recent beginnings, Baker's Graveyard is probably the oldest known burial place in the county." Baker's was near the Mecklenburg County line on Torrence Place near

Snow Creek Methodist Church, established circa 1801 as King's Methodist Episcopal Church, now occupies an 1881 building. *Courtesy of the author.*

the road from Mount Mourne. The original site of Baker's Graveyard is now under Lake Norman. Most fortunately, the headstones were removed to the Centre Church Cemetery in 1961. The oldest marker is for Reverend John Thompson, 1690–1753.

The establishment of schools was coordinated with the establishment of churches and, as P.F. Laugenour insisted, "The determined settlers would have a school built as soon as they had a roof over their own heads!" The Scots were said to be the best educated of all of the "Mulligan's Stew" of pioneer settlers, and two schools of note were under the auspices of the Presbyterian Church. Crowfield Academy, established in 1760, was the first classical school in western North Carolina and called "the log college" by Laugenour. It was established by the nearby Centre Church, although its exact location remains a point of contention, and it is believed to have been less than two miles from the site of Torrence's Tavern and two miles from the Iredell–Mecklenburg County line, near Belmont (the home of Alexander Osborne). Crowfield retains a mystery about it, and a controversy. It lasted until 1780 and is claimed by both Iredell and Mecklenburg Counties as a historic site, marked by a rough boulder that once held a plaque for the 1760s Osborne home.

The second school—named for Clio, the muse of history—was Clio Nursery of Arts and Sciences, established in 1774. It was located between Snow Creek Church and the South Yadkin River and lasted until 1787, when it burned. James Hall, who had been the teacher at Clio, then opened his own school, Hall's Academy, near his home at Bethany. Hall taught Latin, English, "belle lettres," geography, algebra, surveying, navigation, composition, rhetoric and science. His academy was the first school to teach science in the state. Sadly, Hall's Academy was torn down in 1917. P.F. Laugenour stated that there were other classical schools at Thyatira, Poplar Tent, Buffalo, Coddle Creek and Robert Chapman's at the Centre Meeting House.

The Robert Hill log house, circa 1763, is a rare homestead remaining in its original state, with contents intact and still owned by tenth-generation descendants. A part of the once-thriving Liberty Hill community, the house sits in a glade bounded by two creeks, secluded and eerily quiet. The log shack behind the house was built for a young water boy, Black Prince, who asked to come home with Abram Hill after the Revolution. Not believers in slavery, the Hills built the shack for the boy and he worked for bread, board and a little pay. (See Mildred Miller's survey of the remaining log structures in the county, circa 2003, in *Iredell County Tracks*, Vol. XXVI, No. 3.) Another eighteenth-century dwelling is located in Elmwood on the Darshana Plantation in Chambersburg. Built by John McElwraith in 1753, it is the oldest dwelling in the county. The two-story design is similar to Virginia houses of the late 1600s and early 1700s—built of brick on a foundation of granite blocks.

The early Third and Fourth Creek settlers are listed in *Heritage of Iredell County*, Vol. I, published by the Genealogical Society of Iredell County; households are shown on the William Sharpe Map of 1773, which is also reproduced in that volume. Local historian

The Robert Hill log house, circa 1763, still stands on original family-owned land in North Iredell. *Courtesy of the author.*

The John McElwraith house, circa 1753, is the oldest dwelling in the county and is located on the Darshana Plantation. *Courtesy of the author.*

Mildred Miller notes settler's names in northwest Iredell in Vol. I, Article 12, of *Heritage of Iredell County*, and on a map, *The Early Landowner's Map of Iredell County ca. 1700*. Both books and maps are housed in the Local History Room of the Iredell County Library.

Fort Dobbs

There are at present seventy-five families on my lands. I viewed between thirty and forty of them and except two, there were not less than five or six to ten children in each family, each going barefooted and in their shirts in warm weather…they are a colony from Ireland removed from Pennsylvania. Besides these are twenty-two families of German or Swiss, who are all an industrious people.
—Royal Governor Arthur Dobbs, 1755

The years between 1730 and 1776 are categorized as the Royal Colony Years. They ushered in progress as well as conflict in the form of protests over taxation and other Crown policies. These decades heralded the beginnings of towns, churches and the printing press, and included tradesmen such as smiths, tanners, wheelwrights, coopers, weavers and shoemakers. As the British colonies had fewer natural resources than French and Spanish possessions, the reward for settling in the new colonies was land. Thus, while Britain created its own overseas market, it continued to need more and more land. From 1754 until 1763, conflict raged between England and France over territory, in particular control of the Ohio Valley region. This "war for empire" (the French and Indian War) intruded on development in North Carolina with a series of small battles including the Cherokee raid on Fort Dobbs.

In 1754, Royal Governor Arthur Dobbs convinced the General Assembly to equip a company of 150 foot soldiers (militia) to protect the frontier by establishing a fortified site from which they could restrain the Indians "incited to aggressive acts by the French." Governor Dobbs wrote of the fort built between two forks of Fourth Creek on an elevated plateau with clear lines of sight near "the large and beautiful Yadkin River." In 1756, Fort Dobbs was completed. Captain Hugh Waddell, a clerk of the colonial council, was in command and he secured treaties with both the Catawbas and the Cherokees. Fort Dobbs was the only government fort on the North Carolina frontier, but there were other semifortified towns in the greater area. "In the same year and the year following, a great number of people sought refuge with the Moravians who enclosed their town, Bethbara, and the adjacent mill with a palisades." Early

Fort Dobbs, as it will be reconstructed. The Robert Steele painting illustrates the fort as it will be built in the near future. *Courtesy of the Friends of Fort Dobbs.*

historian E.F. Rockwell also listed as semifortified: Beaver Dam at Withrow's Creek; a site near the McKee and Simonton homes on Fourth Creek; east of Captain Eagle near Union Church; Sherrill's Ford Road; Fifth Creek near Andrew Reed's home; and near Murdock's at St. Michael's Church.

Both 1754 and 1755 were calamitous years for the British—with the following two years marking a near-disastrous failure of the British offensive—leading the Indians to attack and plunder settlement after settlement. After the 1758 Forbes's victory, which succeeded in retaking previously lost territory, the advantage turned in favor of the British and the Cherokee Wars (1759-1761) began in earnest. The Indians vigorously executed attacks against the western outposts of southern settlements. The Cherokees were at war in North Carolina by 1760 and alarmed settlers fled to Fort Dobbs, built a small settlement around the fort and remained there for the duration of the war. Early in 1760, the fort itself was attacked by a small band of Cherokees who were repelled by the militia installed there. The Crown launched its own attack against the Cherokees in 1761, going deep into their territory and ultimately ending the hostilities.

A Moravian contingent took one thousand pounds of lead from the stores at Fort Dobbs in 1763, sending a load of pottery in exchange. The General Assembly passed a resolution to move the remaining supplies to Salisbury and the fort was officially closed, but it remained a local place of refuge until the Revolution. In 1767, Waddell commanded an escort for Governor Tryon's expedition to establish definite boundaries for the Cherokees (Tryon succeeded Dobbs, who died in 1765). Fort Dobbs was also used as an arsenal for the troops under Griffith Rutherford during the Cherokee uprising of 1776. There are no stories about the fort after the Revolution. Eventually, the skeleton of the fort burned down; only the mystery remains.

The planned reconstruction of Fort Dobbs will make the site one of only a few recreated forts from this period. It was, at one time, the westernmost military camp in the colonies and the only government fort on the North Carolina frontier. Fort Dobbs was added to the National Register of Historic Places in 1970. The Division of State Historic Sites and the Department of Cultural Resources have committed themselves to its reconstruction and a master plan is now nearing completion.

Military uniforms have been recreated from descriptions found in the 1755 letter from Governor Dinwiddie of Virginia to Governor Dobbs of North Carolina. The location was described when Dobbs gave his report to the General Assembly in 1756, and the fort itself was described in detail in a report made from an inspection conducted in 1756. The written report contained a sketch of the fort; those records were the focus of a search of the office of North Carolina State Archives & History, as well as of archives in England. Dr. Stanley South, an archaeologist formerly at the State Archives & History office, wrote that the mysterious "opposite angles" referred to in early descriptions were probably blockhouses on the corners. Jerry Cashion—formerly with the University of North Carolina–Chapel Hill Department of History—claimed that those angles, so perplexing to previous historians, were merely bastions, common in European forts. Dr. Lawrence Babits of East Carolina University recently evaluated previous archaeological findings and recommended that the reconstruction of the fort commence.

Although archaeological digs in 1969 unearthed over six hundred fragments, at that time only seventy vessels had been identified; almost half of those were considered refined ceramics such as delftware punch bowls, Moravian stoneware and Chinese and English stoneware. Artifacts such as clay pipes, animal bones, glass, lead musket balls, buckshot, spume, swan shot, pistol balls and various hardware and metal clothing parts such as stock buckles and shoe and knee buckles were also among the five thousand items eventually recovered. The dig resulted in a successful outline of the footprint of the fort. The earthwork remains include a moat, cellar, magazine and a well, in addition to architectural features including postholes, a hearth and a ditch.

Even though this "footprint" is all that remains aside from written descriptions and various small relics, dedication to the site has been relatively continuous since 1909, when the Fort Dobbs Chapter of the Daughters of the American Revolution bought ten acres surrounding the site. From the installation of a marker in 1910 until World War I, Fourth of July celebrations were held at the site north of Statesville. In the late 1930s, the DAR built a log chapter house, and in 1973, the site was turned over to the state and an additional twenty acres were purchased.

The mission of the Fort Dobbs State Historic Site is "to preserve and interpret North Carolina's only French and Indian War fort," and to provide a vital historic site with an accurately reconstructed fort. A monument has been erected at Fort Dobbs in honor of Hugh Waddell. Donated by the Society of Colonial Wars, it was dedicated in October of 2007. See www.fortdobbs.org.

Chapter 2

1776–1858

*The War for Independence, the Formation of Iredell County
and Life in the New America*

The Revolutionary War

*The great advantage of the Americans is that they have arrived at a state of democracy without having
to endure a democratic revolution, and that they are born equal without "becoming so."*
—*Alexis de Tocqueville,* Democracy in America

Iredell County was merely a primitive outpost when the Revolution began, and it was still a part of Rowan County, which at that time covered the entire northwestern quadrant of North Carolina. Many of the settlers in the "Western District" were prominent citizens belonging to the Rowan Committee for Safety and to the Continental Congress. Homer Keever wrote in *Iredell, Piedmont County*: "The Rowan Resolves were the most strongly worded of any county resolutions of the time, and earlier than many, even the well known Mecklenburg Resolves, which came one year after Rowan's."

By the year 1775, King George III had proclaimed that the American colonies were "in an open and avowed state of rebellion" and Lord Cornwallis responded with bravado, "Give me four regiments of Regulars and I will march triumphant from one end of the continent to the other." The Cherokees allied themselves with the British and remained adamant in their opposition to the settlers. In July of 1776, the Cherokees attacked colonial settlements, coordinating their attacks with the British assault on Charleston; in September of that same year, the previously mentioned foray against the Cherokees, led by General Rutherford, wiped out much of the tribe. The Cherokee Treaty of 1777 ceded land to the state but restricted entry into Indian hunting grounds. (Obviously, this agreement did not stand because it was 1792 before "Perpetual Peace" was mutually agreed upon.) The War for Independence continued for seven years, 1776–1783.

In early 1781, the "Retreat of Nathanael Greene" traversed the Piedmont on the way to Virginia to regroup and recruit. This done, Greene retraced his steps in the early spring, meeting Cornwallis at Guilford Courthouse and inflicting such punishment that Cornwallis fled to Wilmington. A skirmish at Torrence's Tavern, a country inn at Mount Mourne, was the site of the only confrontation within the future Iredell County. Wheeler wrote that the militia "broke and ran" after killing seven men and twenty horses. Foote wrote, "A small party was attacked and dispersed by British Col. Tarleton." (It is possible,

A Revolutionary War reenactment at the Farmstead at Iredell Museums. *Courtesy of Iredell Museums.*

but Tarleton's troops had previously very nearly been wiped out by Greene's forces, led by Daniel Morgan, at Cowpens in January.) And other sources wrote that all patriots but one ran, leaving their guns at the tavern, with the man remaining having shot a British officer before he fled. Clearly, there is a material difference in the "facts" presented in these stories. Whatever may have happened, there are many war casualties buried at Hopewell Presbyterian Church on the southern county line near the former site of Torrence's Tavern.

As many as one in five colonists preferred to remain subjects of a crown colony and nearly twenty thousand joined loyalist military units. The Patriots called them Tories. Homer Keever wrote in *Iredell, Piedmont County* that the lists of Tories from Rowan County "are bare of Iredell names." However, E.F. Rockwell's 1876 Independence Day address in Statesville declared that "a large district of what was then Rowan was not so friendly to the cause of liberty as might have been desired…[and] following Hunting Creek up to the Brushy Mountains, you would have found inhabitants nearly all Tories throughout the mountains to the Catawba River." Approximately one in thirty former settlers did leave the colonies after the war. Nearly forty thousand resettled in Canada and another forty thousand settled in crown colonies such as India, Jamaica and the Bahamas. More than one thousand African Americans relocated in 1792, from their previous safe harbor in Nova Scotia, to Sierra Leone; and several thousand former slaves who were granted freedom to fight for the British also left the colonies.

The Patriots won their independence, recognized in the Peace Treaty of 1783, and all remaining unclaimed Granville property was confiscated. Thereafter, the State of North Carolina issued grants and claims to settlers. Granville died in England in 1764, at the end of the French and Indian War, and his heirs did not continue the process of granting surveys. Local historian Mildred Miller wrote that at the time of Granville's death, there were only a few grants made north of the South Yadkin in western Iredell. However, settlers had continued to establish homesteads and farms with enthusiasm between the years of 1764 and 1783, even with no grant process to formalize their settlement. When a law was passed by the state to provide for the sale of land, the Rowan Claims Office was overwhelmed by the ensuing rush for land claims.

The tsunami of settlers could not be stopped; it continued with renewed vigor after the war and eventually pushed away all treaty boundaries as the momentum of expansion westward continued even more aggressively. The colonists were quick to take on the identity of "Americans," a term previously accorded the native inhabitants, with colonists referring to themselves according to the country of their birth. These new Americans flaunted their complete freedom from Britain by using Indian names and words. The English language now contains thousands of words taken directly from Indian languages.

The years between 1784 and 1800 would usher in the Federal Period to which North Carolina submitted only reluctantly. The state had initially rejected the new United States Constitution, insisting on a bill of state's rights. It would be nine months before North Carolina joined the United States of America.

The Daughters of the American Revolution was first organized in Mooresville in 1903 and in Statesville in 1908 as the Fort Dobbs Chapter. The Fourth Creek Chapter of the DAR was formed in Statesville in 1959. (Fourth Creek and Fort Dobbs chapters have now merged.) The DAR continues to be the grand dame of historical organizations, promoting preservation and education and offering scholarships to outstanding students annually. The Iredell Society of Colonial Dames was organized in 1933. The Daughters of Colonial Wars was organized in 1939, and in 1940, it set a monument in the median at East Broad and Tradd Streets in Statesville. The Daughters of American Colonists was organized in 1963. The Farmstead at Iredell Museums has featured war encampments and militia musters from the Revolutionary period presented by reenactment groups. A listing of some of Iredell County's Revolutionary War heroes can be found in *Heritage of Iredell County*, Vol. II.

County of Iredell—Town of Statesville

A grove of pines was pointed out to me as the first place hereabouts occupied by buildings of sufficient import to assume the dignity of being called a residence, and this villa or ville (a county seat usually the residence of a wealthy person-Webster) which, from its being on the State Road, naturally took the name Statesville.

—*P.F. Laugenour, 1916* Sentinel

Iredell County was formed on Nov. 18, 1788, when Judge James Iredell, leading the Hillsborough Convention, was to decide if North Carolina would join the newly formed United States. A bill was introduced to divide Rowan County and only passed by a very narrow margin. The name Iredell, for the proposed new county, had been written into the pending bill; thus, Iredell County was born, lying between the Catawba and Yadkin Rivers. The act creating the county can be found in Chapter 36, *Public Law of 1788.* In a second convention of the General Assembly in 1789, Judge Iredell succeeded in providing for North Carolina as the twelfth state of the Union and for Statesville as the county seat of the new county.

Judge Iredell was one of the first North Carolina Superior Court judges (circa 1778), the North Carolina Attorney General in 1779, the Council of State in 1787, and appointed to the United States Supreme Court by George Washington in 1790. The name "Iredell" itself is Old English in origin, dating from the 1066 Battle of Hastings, with "Eyredale" meaning "valley of air." The name also derives from the Aire River valley in northern England.

The choice of the name "Statesville" remains a mystery. E.F. Rockwell surmised that the name came from a state road running through the center of town—from Salisbury, the county seat of Rowan, to the mountains. Homer Keever wrote that there is no evidence of such a road; however, a number of roads did form a network in and around Statesville, including Cove Gap, Island Ford, Shallow Ford, the Great Road (also called the Georgia Road [U.S. 21]) and the (Old) Mountain Road. W.M. Robbins posits that Statesville is named in honor of the state of North Carolina, a newly independent state with a "state's village" as the main town in the new county. Keever agrees with this premise. Others offer that the name grew from agitation over issues of state's rights that arose with the opportunity to become a state within the new United States. Still others maintain that because the town was in the center of Iredell County, as well as the center of North Carolina by cartographers' measurements of the time, it became the "State's Village." Regardless of the provenance, Statesville it became, on nearly sixty-nine acres bought from Fergus Sloan for thirty pounds sterling.

A marker is incorporated in the beautiful dry-stone walls of the Fourth Creek Burying Ground to mark one of the original town boundaries. In 1790, twenty-six lots were sold at auction in the new town and Statesville was empowered to build a prison and stocks. Broad Street, at one hundred feet wide, was appropriately named, as was Center Street, which ran along a ridge through the center of the town. Meeting Street began at the Fourth Creek Meeting House, Tradd Street was said to be a trail and

Judge James Iredell, North Carolina Attorney General (1751–1799) and United States Supreme Court Justice (1790-1799). *Courtesy of Iredell Museums.*

Front Street ran in front of the courthouse, so wrote nineteenth-century historian E.F. Rockwell. (The 1883 *Landmark* stated that town commissioners rescinded the "high sounding names bestowed upon the streets" in 1881. There is no list of these names and the signs were taken down with the streets again referred to by their original names. Another mystery.) The 1961 edition of the *Record and Landmark, Past and Present,* includes a two-page map of early Statesville with buildings sketched in and labeled with the owners and occupants listed. The map, drawn by local artist Edrie B. Knight, is an interesting reference. *Iredell County Landmarks* also contains a map of the residents within the town limits, circa 1790, drawn by Grier Surveying. The Sanborn maps—detailed insurance maps used for reference—can also be consulted on the computers at the Iredell County Library in Statesville.

Fourth Creek Burying Ground with First Presbyterian Church (Statesville) in the background, on the site of the original Fourth Creek Meeting House. *Photograph by Max Tharpe. Courtesy of Mitchell Community College.*

North Carolina, still primarily a farming area, was ambivalent during the early decades of the nineteenth century. The economy plodded along and there was a definite scarcity of cultural advances. The Jefferson years, 1800–1812, saw the beginning of the Antifederalist movement with lower taxes and a nonintrusive Federal government. Homer Keever made an extensive survey of population and businesses in Statesville at that time. Suffice it to say, Statesville was a tiny village with a few houses, three stores, two taverns, seventy-six citizens and six slaves in 1800 (another source lists sixty-eight whites and twenty-seven slaves). In 1790, the Patrick Hughey Tavern sold one half pint of whiskey for one shilling (a nickel) and a quart of beer for eight pence (eight cents). A meal could be enjoyed for one shilling and six pence and a bed for the night for four pence. A quart of corn or oats for two pence and hay for a shilling fed the livestock and mounts (from the 1890 *Landmark*). The county census in 1790 listed 5,435 inhabitants and 858 slaves.

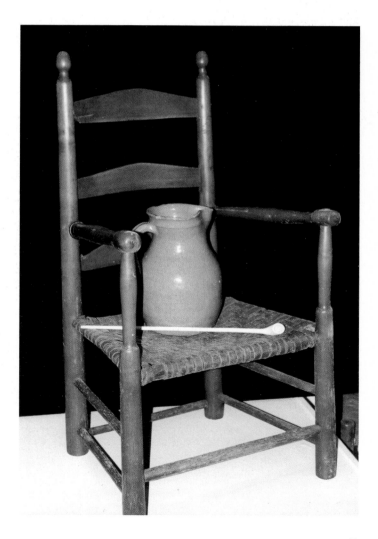

Catawba Valley "tavern pitcher," circa 1700, and a white clay pipe popular in the eighteenth century. *Courtesy of Iredell Museums.*

41

A log courthouse was built in 1790 in the middle of what Statesville now calls the "town square." The court opened in the autumn of 1790, after previously meeting at the Simonton House. *The Inventory of Historic Architecture* dates the Simonton House to circa 1870; it was built of Flemish-bond bricks. Gary Freeze notes in that publication that the brick shell could be eighteenth century but the remainder of the house dates from the 1870 remodel, with other twentieth-century changes. However, he does acknowledge that local tradition insists that the court met there before 1790.

The court appointed all local officials including: road overseer (to verify that residents within two miles of a roadway kept up their part of the road); stray master (charged with penning stray animals until they could be claimed by their owners); entry taker (similar to the register of deeds); and constables, a sheriff and a clerk of court. This was the town government. Quickly outgrown, the log courthouse was relocated to become Muschat Academy and a new two-room brick courthouse was built on the square. At the same time, around 1818, a brick jail was built on East Broad Street and had, according to P.F. Laugenour in the 1915 *Sentinel*, "a whipping post in the yard, a common punishment for larceny and misdemeanors. Brandings, hangings, and burnings were all recorded, but were abolished during Reconstruction," although the last hanging did not take place until 1903.

The Statesville Post Office was established in 1801, and during the early years of Iredell County, small post offices proliferated, handling mail and serving as community

The Simonton House, Statesville, features an eighteenth-century, Flemish-bond brick shell with renovations about 1870 and also in the twentieth century. *Courtesy of the author.*

crossroads and meeting places. A stagecoach carried the mail over a "post road," of which there were eventually five crossing the county. The roads from the period are much the same today, with the Old Mountain Road being the route that has least changed over time. Of course, at the time it was the Mountain Road, and it ran along a ridge that had been traveled since the time of the earliest pioneers. Keever's book, *Iredell, Piedmont County*, contains an excellent review of local post offices as well as a detailed survey of the roads, then and now, expressing how little the major travel routes have changed. Mildred Miller's survey of local post offices can be found in *Heritage of Iredell County*, Vol. I.

Life in the Backcountry

This village [Statesville] *was as dull as hot parching weather could make it…the few gentlemen sitting here and there under the shade trees didn't seem to care if they growed fast to one of Dearman's split bottoms…almost the only thing of life to be seen was a little black pup which amused itself in barking, and answering his own voice, echoed back to him from the massive walls of Simonton House.*
—*J.J. Brunner, Editor,* Carolina Watchman

Statesville in 1834 was described by an editorialist in the 1884 *Landmark* as having "a courthouse in the center of the square" and the Presbyterian Church which "was a log house." The listing continued with "the Methodist Church, the school house, three shoe shops, two tailors, one carriage shop, one carpenter, three blacksmiths, one harness shop, one hatter, three doctors, three attorneys, two hotels, and 'a few loafers!'" The writer counted twenty-six families in the village. However, the 1884 *Landmark* itself listed four doctors, eighteen houses, sixteen shops, ten offices, five warehouses, two hotels and one boardinghouse in 1834 Statesville. Either way, it was a nice village.

John Nisbet's General Store was the first of its kind, located where the clock tower now stands, and provided soap, paper, tobacco, knives, toothbrushes, soda powder, sugar, flannel, lace, buttons, pepper and molasses. Other items in great demand were steel, iron, nails, hoes, plows and furniture. Payment was often made in the form of surplus wheat, oats, flax, seed, wool, hides and pork or beef. The trade that developed was mainly local, dealing in products from farms, most of which were between one and four hundred acres. Some farmers sent their surplus to ports at Charleston or Philadelphia, or to Camden, Cheraw, Salisbury and Charlotte. This practice was called "wagonning"; the wagon, on the return trip, was often laden with merchandise and specialty items from the larger towns.

The chief crops were corn, wheat, oats, hay, potatoes, cotton, tobacco and fruit. Cotton, a minor crop before 1793, began to overtake the tobacco market in the 1820s in a state that had previously been a tobacco colony; when tobacco revenues dropped in the nineteenth century, cotton became the leading cash crop. The larger cotton planters were concentrated in the flatter land of south Iredell while tobacco was grown more often in the north.

Log cabins from Iredell County relocated to the Farmstead at Iredell Museums. *Courtesy of Iredell Museums.*

Farmville Plantation (now Darshana), built circa 1817–1818 by Joseph Chambers in the Federal style with many details that signify the work of Asher Benjamin, a Boston architect. *Courtesy of the author.*

One third of the population held only a few slaves and another third held none. Iredell County was never a large slaveholding area but over two dozen settlers owned over one thousand acres each and a few owned over two thousand acres each; those latter, few planters held twenty or more slaves. Farmville Plantation in Elmwood, now called Darshana, is on the National Register of Historic Places. The house was built by Joseph Chambers in 1817–1818 in the Delaware Valley tradition of Federal design. Farmville was one of the largest plantations in the county. Major Rufus Reid's home, Mount Mourne Plantation, was built in the 1830s on four thousand acres. The house is one of the county's finest examples of a plantation home and is also on the National Register. The Neel House, circa 1830, west of Mooresville (also known as the Cornelius Johnson House), was originally Byers' Springdale Plantation. It began on more than six hundred acres on the Stage Coach Road (Old River Road [U.S. 150]) that came through the property at the back of the house. The Neel House sits amid the rambunctious development along the highway, with the front-and-back perception of the house reversed so that the house now faces the main road. It is also on the National Register.

But the more numerous middle class, dominated by yeoman farmers, lived on small holdings providing only for themselves and their family, producing at home nearly everything they needed except salt, iron, sugar, coffee, spice and fine cloth. There was no dearth of game which included deer, wild turkey, pheasants, hawks, wild geese and ducks, squirrels and the occasional crane and wildcat. Log was the preferred building

Mount Mourne Plantation, a Greek Revival manse built circa 1830 by Major Rufus Reid. Many features allude to the influence of Boston architect, Asher Benjamin, but it is attributed to Jacob Stirewalt, Piedmont master builder. *Courtesy of the author.*

The Cornelius-Johnson House, formerly Byers' Springdale Plantation, circa 1830, is now known as the Neel House. Built of Flemish-bond brick, the early Greek Revival styling is attributed to Jacob Stirewalt, Piedmont master builder. *Courtesy of the author.*

form until around 1876. It did not necessarily indicate poverty or lower status, but rather was a functional and traditional building material in an area rich with good timber. The hearth was the center of the home, providing warmth, light and heat for cooking in these traditional log cabins. Settlers raised and preserved their own food, grew flax for linen, kept sheep for wool, churned butter, made soap and candles, cleared land to cultivate gardens and built their own homes, barns and outbuildings. Even tools and hardware were made at home or by the local smith. Furniture was cobbled together and clothing was sewn by hand. Corn was grown to feed livestock as well as the settlers and they ate corn chowder, cornbread, hominy and grits; they also fed corn to their chickens, turkeys and pigs. An interesting note from E.F. Rockwell stated that the Scots-Irish settlers were more skilled at farming and "domestic manufacture," preferring the staple cornmeal mush; the Marylanders, skilled at agriculture and the "culinary arts," preferred the staple hominy.

The backcountry period saw an increase in the Baptist and Methodist populations, inspired by the "Great Revival" (circa 1800) and often featuring camp meetings. The only two churches in Statesville at the time were Fourth Creek Presbyterian (Statesville Presbyterian circa 1875 but First Presbyterian by the 1890s) and Mount Zion Methodist (Statesville Methodist in 1883, First Methodist by 1902 and Broad Street Methodist by 1907). Bethesda Presbyterian, organized in 1847 and built in 1853 in southeast Iredell in the Amity community, is the oldest church sanctuary in continuous use in the county. It is a two-story Federal and Greek Revival–style building on Bethesda Road. According to Keever, there were fifty-eight pre–Civil War churches in the county. For detailed information on churches, see *Heritage of Iredell County*, Vol. I, pp. 95–145.

The first school charter was given to John Muschat's Statesville Academy in 1814. Classes were held in the old log courthouse that had been moved to make room for the larger, second courthouse. The 1885 *Landmark* wrote, "Between 1815 and 1825 Mr. Muschat established the original Statesville Male Academy standing near the First Presbyterian Church site. It was torn down and moved to David Wallace's lot." A girls' school is said to have held class in the Fourth Creek Meeting House (First Presbyterian); Ebenezer Academy was chartered in 1822 and located in the former session house at Bethany Church. A larger building was built in 1823 and was used as an academy until 1856, then as a public school until 1912. The building was restored in 1913 by the DAR and is the oldest school building still standing in Iredell County.

Education for girls and young women began after 1830, and the Iredell Public School System began in 1839. Schools before this time were privately run. "Field schools" were subscription schools covering elementary subjects, while "academies" provided the equivalent of a high school education and continued to provide the same well into the early twentieth century. The Feimster family set up a tuition-free school for girls at their home near Liberty Hill and it became the first free school in the county; however, most early academies were under the auspices of the Presbyterian Church. The Methodist

Bethesda Presbyterian Church, established in 1847, boasts a simple sanctuary, the oldest still in use in the county. *Courtesy of the author.*

The Ebenezer Academy, circa 1823, is the oldest school building in the county. *Courtesy of the author.*

Church chartered an academy at Snow Creek in 1849 that lasted until it was sold to the Iredell Public School System in 1886.

In Statesville, the Buena Vista Academy on Front Street was founded in the 1850s by the Andrews brothers from South Carolina. It became a military school during the war then functioned as an academy from 1869 until 1874. In 1851, Brantley York and Baxter Clegg organized an Olin academy called New Institute. It was chartered in 1855 as Olin Academy and hoped to become a Methodist college. Named for Stephen Olin, a minister, it was called "the college" and lasted until 1833, its dream unrealized. In 1870, the Statesville Male Academy was chartered and a new building was built on a hill near Armfield and Mulberry Streets. The area is still called "Academy Hill" even though the academy disappeared about 1891 (according to the *Landmark* of that same year) as the graded schools took precedence. The building, renovated as a private home, still stands. Academy Hill, historian Gary Freeze states, "contains the oldest schools, some of the oldest industrial, a group of Late-Victorian houses, a Late-Victorian commercial row, and a Gothic Revival church." For detailed information on schools, see *Heritage of Iredell County*, Vol. I, pp. 64–95, and Laugenour's list of schools, reprinted in *Iredell County Tracks*, Vol. XXIII, No. 3, published by the Genealogical Society of Iredell County.

Abundant power from area streams made possible the proliferation of grain mills and sawmills. The mills along the streams in north Iredell sustained villages such as Turnersburg, Olin and Eagle Mills, with the attendant founding of stores in those areas. From 1800 until the Civil War, numerous mills prospered, and buhr (burr) and oil mills

The Statesville Male Academy, circa 1870 (chartered in 1875), is a one-story Classical Revival building in the Academy Hill Historic District. It is now restored as a private home. *Courtesy of the author.*

were common. The French buhr was a mill improvement brought to Iredell by Jacob Crater in 1849 and quickly adapted by local millers. (A buhr is a hard, siliceous rock used for millstones and whetstones.)

Two large, successful mills were Eagle Mills and Turner Mills at Turnersburg. Eagle Mills, started by the former peddler Andrew Baggerly, opened in 1852 producing yarn and cloth and was the larger of the two mills. However, Baggerly lost his interest in the mill due to bankruptcy and his dream of an industrial center, Eagle City, failed. The Turner Mill, which had been the 1847 Notley Tomlin cotton mill on Rocky Creek, was bought by Wilfred Turner in 1856, adding weaving to the yarn mill in 1860. The workers formed the mill village of Turnersburg. The Turner family home was built in 1812 as a two-story log house. It has since been covered with weatherboard and greatly expanded with front porches, wings and additions to the original structure. It is currently operated as a private enterprise. Iredell Museums has a large collection from the Turner family, including photographs and ledgers from the Turner Stores (see Articles 41, 43, 52, 53 and 218 in Vol. 1 of *Heritage of Iredell County*).

The Farmstead at Iredell Museums includes a reconstructed one-room school that is frequently the site of demonstrations of backcountry schooling, including a turn on the dunce stool if necessary. Reenactors regularly illustrate daily life as well, with "Spring Planting," "Harvest Day," "Christmas at the Cabins" and other living history events. The Farmstead itself is a medley of cabins and outbuildings relocated from other parts of Iredell and carefully reconstructed. The collection includes an 1890 corncrib, a

The Turner Homeplace was the birthplace of W.D. Turner, lieutenant governor of North Carolina under Governor Aycock in the early twentieth century. The front portion of the house, circa 1818, is the much-altered original log construction. *Courtesy of the author.*

blacksmith shop, the Renegar log house, the 1870–1880 Thompson cabin (now a barn), the watering trough that had been used at the 1854 courthouse, the Templeton cabin and the smokehouse from a plantation near the site of Torrence's Tavern that dates from pre-Revolution years. The centerpiece of the site is the meticulously reconstructed Sharpe cabin, circa 1790, formerly located on Midway Road. Iredell Museums has a large collection of early implements, tools and plows, and a hand-hewn barn loom on the site. (Lewis Alexander, an independent preservationist, has also personally rescued a number of log buildings in the county and reconstructed them at his home farm on County Line Road.)

Rural isolation ended around the time of the "great fire" that burned most of the town west of Center Street, as well as the courthouse on the square. The fire razed two-thirds of the town in December of 1854 (some sources state 1855; regardless, it was the first of several fires that nearly engulfed downtown, resulting in most current buildings dating between 1860 and 1930). The courthouse was destroyed but almost all of its records were saved. The exuberant young town of Statesville recovered, rebuilding a new courthouse within months.

The third courthouse was built between 1855 and 1856 on South Center Street, featuring an attractive balcony with a curving double exterior staircase and four large two-story columns. Construction had also begun on the centerpiece of the town,

Open-hearth cooking at the Farmstead at Iredell Museums. *Courtesy of Iredell Museums.*

A historic reenactment from the "backcountry" at the Farmstead. *Courtesy of Iredell Museums.*

The Harry Mott House, circa 1858–1875, was built by the Houston family in the Late Greek Revival style. By 1880, it was occupied by the Mott family and has undergone alteration. *Courtesy of the author.*

Daltonia (near Harmony) an 1858 Italianate Revival plantation house built by John Dalton, is still in the family today. *Courtesy of the author.*

Mitchell College, originally named Concord Presbyterian Female College. The charter was granted in July of 1853 to the Concord Presbytery and construction began in the fall of 1854. Mitchell Professor William Moose has written a comprehensive history of the college, *A History of Mitchell Community College*, and it is informative and delightful—a fitting tribute to the beautiful old main building that stands as a crowning glory at the end of West Broad Street. The building is listed on the National Register.

Plantation houses continued to be built in the county. Mount Mourne, near Mooresville, is an area that was nearer to plantation life in the traditional sense and antebellum homes still stand there. The Harry Mott House was built in 1858 by James Franklin Houston, who lived in a log cabin while the imposing two-story house with classic columns was being built. Henry Mott moved into the main house in 1880 and the house remains in the family today. In north Iredell, Houstonville was also a community of plantations where one of the first schools, Harmony Hill Academy, was established. Daltonia, north of Harmony near Houstonville, was built in 1858 and named for John H. Dalton who built the Italianate Revival plantation house. Dalton had the largest rural tobacco factory in the county before the Civil War. Daltonia is still in the family today. The log house on the property was the family home until the "big house" was built. Both plantation houses are on the National Register. *The Inventory of Historic Architecture*, by Stokes and Freeze, lists fourteen former plantations in Iredell that are examples of antebellum architecture.

Chapter 3

1858–1900

The New Country at War and the Emerging Markets Created
by the Advent of the Railroad

The Railroad

After I left Charlotte, I traveled over a little railroad that runs, or walks, or pokes along from Charlotte
to Statesville. The road is forty-two miles short and six hours long.

—*1884* Landmark

The era known as the Great Awakening began in 1829 and continued until 1862. North Carolina's reform movement nearly spanned the decade of the 1830s and introduced reform of the state constitution and a tremendous surge of railroad construction. A new political party, the Whigs, advocated education and infrastructure improvements; a free school system debuted in 1839–1840. The news was available daily from the Salisbury newspaper and Eugene Drake quoted market prices in the *Iredell Express* weekly in Statesville. The stagecoach from Salisbury stopped in Statesville. Plank roads were an innovation but the railroad rendered plank roads redundant and ended extensive plans for the roads almost as soon as they had begun.

The 1883 *Landmark* described 1851 Statesville as "a very small place having five stores, a hotel, a tavern, a tan yard, three doctors, and twenty-eight homes." However, Homer Keever details the town as a small town of ministers, teachers, attorneys, physicians and sixteen merchants including tailors, hatters, cabinetmakers, four coopers, a chair maker, a gunsmith, a bookshop, a cotton gin, three masons, twenty-eight carpenters and many blacksmiths (population numbering around 215). Wagon shops and distilleries were prolific, and wheelwrights, millwrights, tanners, shoemakers, harness makers and saddlers were in the forefront of local tradesmen. The county population was almost fifteen thousand and nearly 30 percent slave, with only thirty free blacks.

In the fall of 1858, the Western North Carolina Railroad came to Statesville from Salisbury. The Western route ran from Salisbury to Statesville and Morganton and then on to Asheville. The 1888 *Landmark* quoted train ticket prices as the following: $2.35 to Asheville, $6.00 to Morehead City, $3.10 to Hot Springs and $7.00 to Norfolk. Suddenly released from isolation, Statesville was propelled into the epicenter of trade in cotton, tobacco and liquor, and her newly freed markets began to flourish. The quiet backcountry, shut away from the greater world and becalmed for over half

The Statesville Depot, circa 1910. *Courtesy of the Greater Statesville Chamber of Commerce.*

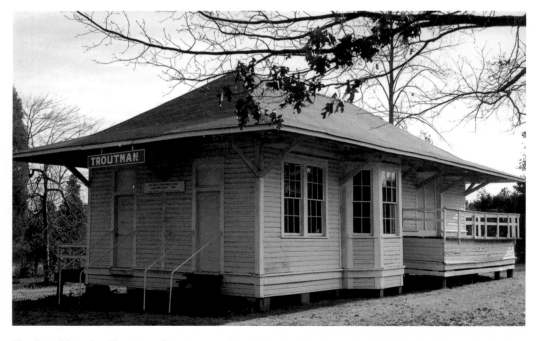

The Late Victorian Troutman Depot, now relocated to the Troutman Family Historical Grounds. *Courtesy of the author.*

a century, no longer existed. A new era began and Statesville enthusiastically handled trade from over a dozen counties as well as receiving twice daily mail delivery to the twenty-nine post offices in the area, which had previously been serviced only once a week by stagecoach.

A few years later, the second railroad connection from Charlotte came into Statesville. The Atlantic, Tennessee and Ohio Railroad reached Statesville in the spring of 1863. This Charlotte–Statesville–Lenoir route was a part of the Western but was dubbed the AT&O, becoming the local rail of choice, and the village of Mooresville became a stop on this line. Bill Arp, writing for the *Atlanta Constitution*, called the AT&O "forty-four miles short and forty-four hours long." It was constantly the object of jokes and said to be "governed by the Quaker Rule," meaning that it did not start "until the spirit moved it!" The railroad was also nicknamed "blackberry road," alluding to the slowness of the train and hinting that one could get off, pick blackberries beside the track and board again with no problem. The 1897 *Landmark* quoted Joe Turner writing for the *Raleigh Sentinel*, "If a hen had laid only nine eggs, Captain Crutchfield's train would wait until she had laid three more so that the farmer might have an even dozen to send to the market at Charlotte." When the AT&O was later extended to Taylorsville, it was dubbed the "June bug" (actually becoming known as such, rather than the AT&O, or, as it was also known, the Statesville and Western). The nickname June bug originated with R.Z. Linney, who proposed a bill for the extension of the line to Taylorsville, saying, "There are green gems [hiddenite] there so valuable a June-bug could carry away $10,000.00 worth!" The AT&O was torn up almost immediately and the iron impressed for military usage during the ensuing Civil War. It was not rebuilt until 1871.

The Civil War

How does God have the heart to allow it?
—*Sidney Lanier, Confederate poet*

The struggle that divided the young country, still less than a century old, began with the April 1861 attack on Fort Sumter. The conflict raged until Lee's surrender at Appomattox Courthouse in April of 1865, but sporadic fighting continued in outlying areas as the death throes of the failed Confederacy lingered. This catastrophic war left a scarred country, bitter for decades, with a death toll of over six hundred thousand men, equaling the combined losses in all other wars from the Revolution to the Korean War.

There were many causes of the War Between the States, but initially it grew from the distinct differences in the land, climate and natural resources of two very different areas of the United States—the agrarian South and the industrial North. When the United States Constitution was written, agriculture was the main occupation, but by 1812, industrial concerns and the population of the northern states were growing steadily. The Compromise of 1850 further divided the country and the election of Lincoln in 1861, giving the North control of the government, resulted in the immediate secession of seven states, with four more to secede after Lincoln's call for government troops to fight the "rebellion" at Fort Sumter.

Iredell County clearly did not want war and its delegates and legislature consistently opposed the proposed 1861 secession. However, when Lincoln called for 750,000 volunteers to suppress the rebellion, Iredell County and the state of North Carolina no longer hesitated to join the Southern Confederacy, and did so on May 20, 1861. Professor William Moose wrote, "Desertion was prevalent among North Carolina troops. In fact, North Carolina had more deserters than any other Confederate state." In 1863, Colonel Silas A. Sharpe was charged with breaking up a large contingent of deserters operating out of the Brushy Mountains in north Iredell. It is important to note that North Carolina had more loss of life than any other state, and that over six hundred men with Iredell connections died during the war. North Carolina's political leaders consistently pressed for withdrawal, with the state legislature openly critical of the war. It is also worth noting that there were crop failures in 1863, creating desperate situations at home and making the urge to go home even more poignant. For a partial list of Confederate veterans, see *Heritage of Iredell County*, Vol. II.

In March of 1865, Sherman defeated General Joseph Johnston's troops at the ill-fated Battle of Bentonville, the most disastrous (and bloodiest) battle fought on North Carolina soil. There were over four thousand dead, Confederate and Union alike. The following month, the governor of North Carolina, the Honorable Zebulon B. Vance, left Raleigh as Union troops advanced on the capitol and retired to Statesville to join his family in what we now call the Vance House.

A large Confederate encampment, circa 1863. *Courtesy of the Statesville Historical Collection of Dr. Steve Hill.*

Statesville saw no military action until the closing days of the war, when General George Stoneman marched into town on April 13, 1865, four days after Lee's surrender. The December 1882 issue of the *Landmark* described the "invasion," writing: "Shortly after dark, several shots were fired from the square by an advance guard and after this all became quiet." The ominous quiet was highlighted by picket lines around the town and by the fact that all houses were "visited" and many looted. After midnight, in the dark hours of the morning of April 14, five thousand Union troops made camp on the forecourt of Mitchell College, then Concord Presbyterian Female College, which had remained open during the conflict. College President Caldwell had hastily decamped from Rome, Georgia, to avoid Sherman's march, coming to Statesville to take the post of president of the college, only to find that Stoneman and his men were soon bivouacked on his campus. William Moose reported in *A History of Mitchell Community College* that the fires in Salisbury could be seen from the cupola of the main building and that the arrival of troops was anticipated with dread.

The policy of the Union army was to burn cotton and supplies, but it is recorded that they burned, raided and looted. The *Iredell Express* newspaper was burned as well as a nearby home; both depots and their supply-filled sheds were burned. The railroad between Statesville and Salisbury was destroyed and the raid on Eagle Mills destroyed the general store, smith, the gristmill, cotton mills and homes of workers. A December 1, 1882 issue of the *Landmark* reported, "[Soldiers] took freedom of the city and ransacked every house, broke into every store, took every good mount." Union troops also overran north Iredell, "confiscating" horses, cattle, silver and other items they deemed of value.

Confederate reenactors at the Farmstead. *Courtesy of Iredell Museums.*

A 1918 edition of the *Landmark* wrote that Stoneman's notorious deserters, Wade and Simmons, terrorized county towns and homes as well.

Governor Vance had relocated his family to Statesville in February of 1865, to a small house near the college. The house was built around 1832, partially of logs, and at the time of Vance's occupation, it served as the official state capitol. It was said that Vance's wife received courteous treatment from Stoneman's raiders; however, Colonel William Palmer had to order the return of personal items that were taken from Mrs. Vance's trunks. Other sources state that the Vance House was stripped of everything and that Statesville residents later refurnished it with items from their own households. Governor Vance and his family remained in the house until May 13.

The *Greensboro Daily News* noted in 1927 that Statesville had been selected for the governor's retreat because "it was considered an out of the way place, off the beaten line of travel. The two railroads that connected the town to the outside world and the telegraph line had been destroyed, therefore Statesville was selected as a refuge for the governor without a government." Governor Vance was arrested in mid-May of 1865 at the Vance House by Federal troops. The governor was then summarily escorted to Salisbury where he was put on a train heading to the Old Capitol Federal Prison in Washington.

The Iredell County Library preserves the personal memoirs, letters and journals of the Civil War, which includes the Civil War letters of Thomas W. Gaither, John

The Historic Vance House and Civil War Museum in Statesville. *Courtesy of the author.*

Burgess Gaither and Mollie D. Gaither, as well as "Ellie's Book," a journal kept by Ellie M. Andrews from 1862 to 1865. Several books are also in the Civil War Collection, including *Recollections of the Civil War*, by J.A. Stikeleather of Olin; *Sketches of the Civil War, Co.'s A, C, & H and the Fourth Regimental Band*, by J.C. Steele; and *Iredell County Soldiers in the Civil War*, by W.N. Watt.

The Historic Vance House and Civil War Museum was relocated from the original West Broad Street site to 501 West Sharpe Street in Statesville; the United Daughters of the Confederacy and the chamber of commerce established the house as a historic site. It is the only former home of Governor Vance that still stands—all others have been destroyed. In 1942, the North Carolina Division of the UDC resolved to secure the house as a state shrine and in 1951, the General Assembly passed a bill enabling them to receive donations for the acquisition and preservation of the house. Artifacts in the house include furnishings from the period, photographs, books and letters. The model of a bronze of Vance fashioned by Gutson Borglum, the sculptor who created Mount Rushmore, is on display. The house is funded by donations and run through the organization Friends of the Vance House.

The United Daughters of the Confederacy was organized in Iredell in 1898, and its first project was the installation of the Confederate Monument on the Old Courthouse lawn, presented to the county by Hurst Turner Post No. 65 of the American Legion, in honor of war mothers. It was dedicated on Mother's Day in 1945. In Mooresville, the UDC is represented by the Battle of Bentonville Chapter. In 1961, a second chapter of the UDC was organized in Statesville. The UDC formally reopened the Vance House to coincide with the centennial of the Confederate Monument installation.

The Sharpe House, another landmark, is the former home of Silas A. Sharpe, who was lieutenant colonel in the Fifty-Second North Carolina and colonel of the Home Guard Militia, as well as the first mayor of Statesville and owner of the largest tan yard in town. Originally a self-sustaining farm, the property has diminished in size due to its downtown location on South Center and Sharpe Streets. The house, circa 1860, is an example of Classical Revival styling and was begun before the war but completed afterward. It has been kept in immaculate condition because of the endowment established by Sharpe's granddaughter, Katherine Nooe Knox. The endowment is today governed by a board of trustees that maintains the property, overseeing its restoration and contents that reflect the original materials and furnishings. A number of portraits are on view and the house is furnished with original pieces as well as period reproductions. Special events and period reenactments have been held at the house and plans for the future provide for even greater access to this Statesville treasure. Local historian O.C. Stonestreet recounts a legend that tells of a bullet, fired by troops during Stoneman's raid, supposedly lodged in the lintel above the front door of the house. The 1882 *Landmark* relates the same story.

A Civil War–era cemetery was found within the last decade when grading began for new construction on U.S. 21 in Statesville; eighty-five gravesites were identified. A local archaeologist surveyed and recorded the site. Wake Forest University conducted excavations. Rough fieldstone had been used for all of the graves at the site, a common

The United Daughters of the Confederacy honor war casualties at the Old Fourth Creek Burying Ground. *Courtesy of the author.*

The Sharpe House in downtown Statesville was the home of Silas A. Sharpe, the first mayor of the town. *Courtesy of the author.*

practice at the time even for larger headstones. Because of the location of the cemetery and a roughly inscribed "A" on one of the stones, it was assumed that at least part of the area was a slave cemetery for the Allison Plantation, formerly located nearby. A local funeral home removed the soil, placed it in coffins (there were no remains) and provided transportation for reburial. Iredell Museums recovered many of the smaller headstones, which were placed in a fenced area on museum grounds. A rededication and consecration of the site was held in 2001.

Freed slaves established their own congregations after the war. The first to form a church were from the Bethany Presbyterian congregation; they organized the first African American church to serve the Southeast, Freedom Presbyterian, circa 1865. It was organized by a Scottish missionary and abolitionist, Sidney Murkland, who had been the pastor at Bethany and who was succeeded by Amos Billingsley, another activist during Reconstruction. Logan Church was organized in 1866 at Scotts with the help of Concord Presbyterian Church; in 1869, Mount Pleasant was built on Center Street near the depot (Center Street AME Zion by 1897). In 1880, Shiloh was built in the Belmont area and two AME Zion churches were organized in Rocky Creek. In 1870, Zion Wesley was organized in Troutman, Watkin's Chapel and Steward's Chapel in Mooresville (circa 1872) and Scotts Chapel in Statesville. In 1874, First Baptist was organized at Garfield Street and became known as Emmaus, moving to Green Street in 1883 and taking the name First Baptist in 1893. Mount Nebo Church was organized in 1870.

A writing desk for the lady of the house; the Sharpe House, Statesville. *Courtesy of the author.*

A rough gravestone from the former Allison Plantation, 1807–1913, Statesville. *Courtesy Iredell Museums.*

Mount Pleasant Church, circa 1869, renamed Center Street AME Zion Church, circa 1897, Statesville. *Courtesy of the author.*

Keaton's Grove near Liberty Hill and St. James's Baptist in Troutman were organized in 1874 and New Friendship Baptist in 1896.

After 1865, the North Carolina Constitution required that the county be divided into townships. Sixteen were chosen since there had been sixteen earlier militia (or captain's) districts. The list of townships was published in the *Landmark* on July 12, 1910, by A.L. Barringer and is included in the Laugenour papers as well. The townships are named for post offices, businesses, churches and former muster districts. Townships include: Eagle Mills, Union Grove, New Hope, Turnersburg, Olin, Sharpesburg, Cool Spring, Bethany, Concord, Chambersburg, Statesville, Shiloh, Barringer, Fallstown, Coddle Creek and Davidson. (Fallstown, Sharpesburg and Davidson were named to honor prominent families.) These townships still exist, but now we think of the county in terms of its municipalities, which are Statesville, Mooresville, Troutman, Harmony and Love Valley.

The following span of time, 1866–1877, was known as Reconstruction. This rebuilding lasted eleven years, according to history timelines, but it lasted much, much longer in reality.

The Iredell Blues

God bless the Tar Heel Boys!

–General Robert E. Lee

The Iredell Blues were officially the Fourth North Carolina State Troops, Company A, and were commissioned as a state and county militia in 1840. Colonel John M. Young was the organizer and commander of what was then called the Independent Iredell Blues, having thirty to forty men enlisted. When the Civil War began, the Blues were actually the first group from Iredell to volunteer, and joined the Fourth North Carolina State Troops, becoming known as Company A. The second group to volunteer was from Andrew's Buena Vista Military Academy in Statesville. They became known as the Saltillo Boys. The third group to volunteer was from north Iredell.

The Blues, Company A, "Iredell's Own", stayed together as a regiment known as Company H for the duration of the war, mostly fighting in eastern North Carolina and Virginia. At least 1,800 Iredell men served the Confederacy. More men from North Carolina died during the war than from any other state. It was said that, "The Iredell women were almost all in mourning since no county suffered more in the loss of her best and bravest sons in the Confederate Army."

The Blues were again called for service when U.S. troops were sent to Mexico to capture Poncho Villa. A 1951 column, "Reminiscing," quotes from an 1898 publication, writing, "The Iredell Blues were in the armory burnishing up accoutrements in anticipation of a call to arms. The company now numbers about sixty. Col. Armfield thinks that if the company is called out, a regiment could easily be recruited." In 1917, they were mobilized for the war in Europe, World War I, and were absorbed into the 30th Old Hickory Division. The 81st Division was known as the "Wildcats," and the artillery from Mooresville was called Battery F of the 113th Field Artillery. During World War I, ninety-two men, whose names are listed in *Heritage of Iredell County*, Vol. I, were men of the Iredell Blues. After the war, the seventy-five-year-old Blues were reactivated as the National Guard, now a cavalry company. In 1938, they were reformed into an engineering unit and again absorbed into the 30th Division.

The Iredell Blues Allison Woods Skirmish Team is today operated by the Stephen Dodson Ramseur Sons of Confederate Veterans Camp and the United Daughters of the Confederacy. Organized in 2001, the team joined the North/South Skirmish Association. The home of the Blues is called Fort Allison in Statesville at Allison's Woods, where they have one of the largest live-fire firing ranges in the South. Live-fire competitions are held using Civil War weaponry such as the musket, carbine, revolver and mortar. The Blues have already won national medals in team and individual competitions, and many members are descendants of the original men of the Iredell Blues.

The group also presents "Living History Weekends" at Allison's Woods, where the area is remade as a nineteenth-century village, complete with craftsmen and artisans. Recent features included a baseball game using 150-year-old rules, a period wedding

The Confederate Monument at the Old Courthouse, Statesville, on Confederate Memorial Day. *Courtesy of the author.*

A Robert Steele painting of the Fourth North Carolina Regimental Band. *Courtesy of Mr. John Steele.*

and reenactments of famous battles. Iredell Museums has a large collection of military items from the Civil War and both World Wars.

The Town of Mooresville

Citizens in Mooresville have a habit of staking their cows in Willow Grove Cemetery. The Mooresville Town Commissioners have instituted a $2.00 fine for anyone continuing to do so.
—from the 1883 Town Records of Mooresville, reprinted by The Historical News

The Atlantic, Tennessee and Ohio rail beds were rebuilt in June of 1871. Its arrival in Iredell sparked the establishment of the second major town in the county, Mooresville. Although Williamsburg was incorporated in 1815 as Iredell's second town, and Olin incorporated in 1852 as the third town ("New Institute"), neither could compete with Mooresville after the railroad came to the town. The Western North Carolina Railroad, whose rails were also removed for the war in 1863, was reopened in 1872 by the Richmond and Danville Line, who bought the bankrupt Western and the rebuilt AT&O as well.

Although the village was founded in the 1850s, it did not come of age until 1873. John Franklin Moore, local businessman and landowner, gave land for the railroad depot and a siding from his large five-hundred-acre tract in 1856; thus, the village was called Moore's Siding, incorporated in 1873, with a population of twenty-five (another source counts twenty-eight families within town limits). Moore offered to sell lots from his large parcel of land to anyone interested in establishing a town, with the one-acre depot site as the center. The railroad tracks ran through the village, between what would become Main and Broad Streets.

Mooresville, in the Coddle Creek Township (the western part of Mooresville has now grown into Davidson Township as well), was a town of general stores focused on farm implements, fertilizer and dry goods. The cotton and corn industries were prospering in the area but Mooresville remained only a local trading center with a drugstore, two doctors, a sawmill run by a steam engine and, in the 1880s, a merchant mill grinding wheat on the share system. The economy was built on Moore's store, cotton gins, commerce from the surrounding neighborhoods and the rail siding at the depot. In 1871, the population was between forty and fifty, with the town having two small dry-goods stores and a "whiskey saloon" near the depot. By 1885, the *Mooresville Monitor* published ads for a barber, two livery stables, three grocers, a watchmaker and jeweler, a hardware store, a saddle shop, a hotel, one store selling furniture, bedding and coffins, a building supplier and a real estate agent.

John Franklin Moore—proprietor of Moore, McLean & Co.—located his business on the public road, the wagon road that was the main street of town. It is said that he insisted on the curve in the wagon road because he could sit on his front porch and see his store on Main Street, which was across from the depot. When new railroad beds were dug (1886–1892), the town wanted to straighten Main Street but landowners would not give permission. The curve remains today, as it was when the wagon road passed through town. In 1885, the Mooresville Town Board ordered a street, fifty feet wide, to be opened from the railroad crossing at Brawley's to the Statesville Road. That is the Oak Street of today. Statesville Avenue remained a wagon road until 1893.

Mooresville was also an academy town. An early school called North Bend was established in 1845 near the depot. It was also the site of Baptist and Methodist meetings. The Presbyterian Mooresville Academy, established in 1874 on Moore-donated land, was the first classical school in the area and presaged the Mooresville Graded School District. It was located on West Moore and South Academy Streets, where the old Central School once stood. The Oak Institute and the Mooresville Academy, operated by Augustus Leazar and Stephen Frontis, were the primary academies in the area. The Methodist Oak Institute burned down around 1893. The Mooresville Female Academy below the Oak Institute became known, after the fire, as the Institute (circa 1900). The Mooresville Academy burned around that time as well.

The First Presbyterian Church and the Methodist Church were both built on Moore-donated land. The First Presbyterian Church was organized in 1875 and 1876 with nineteen members from Prospect Church; it met at the Mooresville Academy until the first church was built at Church and McLelland Streets. The current church, a brick Gothic Revival building, was built in 1899 on McLelland and Academy Streets. The Methodist Church on Moore land was formed in 1877 and later called Central Methodist Church. Reid Memorial Presbyterian Church is the oldest African American congregation in Mooresville, established in 1876.

The AT&O Depot in Mooresville, now the Depot Visual Arts Center. *Courtesy of the author.*

The First Presbyterian Church in Mooresville, established in 1875–1876, and built in 1899 in the Gothic Revival style. *Courtesy of Ms. Cynthia Jacobs.*

John Franklin Moore was buried on his own land. That parcel was purchased from his widow to begin the Willow Valley Cemetery in 1877. John Franklin Moore, the man who gave so much to the town, was the first person buried in Willow Valley. Today, it is the final home of the graves of many Confederate soldiers. It is also the resting place of the Honorable Augustus Leazar, who began the Mooresville Academy in 1874, founded and coedited one of Mooresville's first newspapers (the *Iredell Gazette*) and coauthored a bill to establish the North Carolina College of Agriculture and Mechanical Arts, now North Carolina State University. The Willow Valley Cemetery is on the corner of Church and McLelland Streets and a map is available at the Mooresville Public Library giving the locations of gravesites. O.C. Stonestreet has written a brief biography of Leazar in *Heritage of Iredell County*, Vol. I.

The first Mooresville newspaper was the *Gazette*, lasting from about 1877 until 1881. The *Mooresville Monitor* appeared in 1885 and the *Register*, *Recorder* and the *Iredell Record* were all established in the late 1880s. The "first newspaper of real substance" was the *Mooresville Enterprise*, established in 1899 and continuing until 1947. The *Mooresville Times* had become the *Times-Record* by the turn of the twentieth century. Tom McKnight bought the *Rounder* in 1935 and the *News Leader* in 1940, changing the name of the latter to the *Mooresville Tribune*. The office of the *Tribune* has microfilm from the 1940s of the *Enterprise* and the *Tribune*, and has bound copies up to 1955 as well as newspapers from 2003 on CD.

Willow Valley, the Mooresville town cemetery, established in 1877. *Courtesy of the author.*

The Mooresville Post Office opened in the summer of 1871, but rural delivery did not commence until 1903. In 1876, two night police were hired and each paid fifty cents a week. The first public well in Mooresville opened in 1881 and kerosene streetlamps were soon installed, lasting until Southern Power put in electric lights about 1907. In 1885, the Mooresville telegraph line opened. The town established a hook and ladder company to fight fires in 1885; however, they still worked by lantern light in 1887. John Randall McCorkle, John R. McLelland and S.W. Stevenson practiced medicine in early Mooresville. Goodman Drug opened in 1895 at 101 Main Street, and it was the only drugstore in town for many years. Mooresville was becoming a comfortable place; within two years, an attorney and deputy sheriff were added to the growing population, which advanced from under fifty in 1873 to four or five hundred people by 1890.

In 1889, Statesville organized its first chamber of commerce, primarily to help with the acquisition of railroad routes and the North Carolina Midlands Railroad opened in the spring of 1899. Its route ran from Mooresville to Mocksville and Winston, then to Virginia. The public road became Main Street and Center Avenue became the first crossing street. In 1890, the first hotel was opened as the Johnston Hotel, at 125 North Main Street, by the widow Melchor. The site was home to her father Cyrus Johnston, and was later enlarged and bricked. (It was renamed the Central Hotel and also operated as the Flower's Hotel.) Nat Johnston, a grocer in 1894, had the first ice plant and the first coal dealership. He also made coffins upstairs over the grocery. On a happier note,

The former Goodman Drug Store building, established in 1895, was built with red pressed brick, featuring a rounded corner. *Courtesy of the author.*

bicycles made an appearance in 1894, with the caveat of a ten-mile-per-hour speed limit on sidewalks. Getting a haircut on Sunday was still a misdemeanor and a fine!

The former Big Oak Roller Mill, circa 1887, was named for a giant oak tree that stood in its yard. The oak was said to be an old Indian meeting place and later a shady wayside stop for the stagecoach. By 1899, it was White Oak Mill, a steam-powered roller mill. When the White Oak Mill was sold in 1914, it became Mooresville Flour Mills, which is still operating today as Bay State Milling Company on Main Street. However, textiles soon became the irresistible force that moved the Mooresville economy, with the 1893 shift to manufacturing when Mooresville Cotton Mill was established (becoming Mooresville Mills, Inc. in 1966). In spite of the 1893 panic that set back businesses and the economy in general, plans for the cotton mill advanced and it began operations in 1894. By 1896, the mill had produced over one million yards of cloth and almost two hundred thousand pounds of yarn. By 1916, the original mill was expanded with the addition of Mill No. 2 and Mill No. 3 on South Main Street. In 1916, mill houses were built for workers and Mill No. 4 and Mill No. 5 were added to the complex.

Southern Railway, who had taken over the Richmond and Danville rail lines, completed the last railroad to come to Mooresville via Barber Junction; another institution, then and now, in the heart of Mooresville's Main Street was founded—D.E. Turner's Hardware Store. The Turner brothers first opened on Broad Street in 1899 and in 1900 moved to Main Street, where the store operates today. It has changed little on the outside and the interior is as it has always been and boasts of never having been remodeled. It is filled from the floor to the rafters with necessities and curiosities on wooden shelves, providing a turn-of-the-century feel, and the pleasant echo of footfalls on the old wood floors add to the ambience. Mike Lassiter's new book, *Our Vanishing Americana: A North Carolina Portrait*, features Turner's Hardware, and is recommended for a look at this Mooresville institution. The oldest commercial building was occupied by D.K. McNeely and Sons, 1890–1919. It is now the home of H&R Block in a ubiquitous building in the middle of Main Street.

In 1904, there were ninety-eight telephones in town but the first telephone book was a single sheet having thirty-one subscribers listed. Groceries advertised in the 1905 *Enterprise* were unbelievably priced, with eggs at ten cents a dozen, butter at twelve cents a pound, country ham at fourteen cents a pound, fryers and hens at six and eight cents a pound and wheat at eighty-five cents a bushel. Mooresville in 1907 included the following enterprises: ten grocers, eight meat markets, two hardware stores, two drugstores, three livery stables, two roller mills and ten dry goods stores. There were also two barbers, two hotels, two lawyers, one dentist, five doctors, one newspaper, one library, four brickyards, three cotton mills and gins, one cottonseed oil mill, one sawmill, one bank, one loan and trust, two furniture stores and two factories (one for furniture and one for trousers). There were electric lights from Southern Power, a local telephone service and two real estate agencies. It was a thoroughly "modern" town.

In 1907, the cornerstone was laid for the Mooresville Graded School District at what would be the Central School. The school was destroyed by fire in 1932, but by 1935, the new Central High School was built at West Moore and Academy Streets. In the early

D.E. Turner hardware store in Mooresville today, virtually unchanged for over a century.
Courtesy of the author.

The original Turner Brothers hardware store in Mooresville on Main Street, circa 1900. *Courtesy of the Mooresville Historical Society.*

1900s, Mooresville High School had graduated its first class, which at that time only included grades up to the eleventh grade.

The population of Mooresville was four thousand. W.J. Haselden wrote in *Mooresville, the Early Years* of a passenger on the AT&O, coming into Mooresville in 1917, who asked the conductor, "What is the population of this town?" It is said that the conductor answered, "When we arrive, look out the window and count them. They will all be at the depot." It seems that the trains remained a spectator sport well into the 1930s and 1940s, with "train time" that signaled townspeople to stop whatever they were doing and watch the train roll in!

The Village of Troutman

You can sit in a room made by Troutman, on a chair made in Troutman, sip a mint julep made in Troutman, smoke a brierwood made in Troutman, listen to a radio made in Troutman, then mingle with the happy carefree people made up in Troutman!

—W.D. Troutman, 1934

Troutman was a small community, located in the center of the township of Fallstown, and thickly settled with prosperous farmers. The little village (population: 150) had three churches, two doctors and a post office. The town was connected to, and identified by, the wagon shop of Annie Troutman and her sons, Jacob and Sidney, who came in 1853 to an unpopulated area described at the time as "virgin forest." Their shop was located on the road from Wilkesboro to Charleston, the longest road in Iredell County, now known as U.S. 115, following much the same route as it did then. Troutman, Iredell's "biggest little town," grew up because of (and around) the railroad; it was actually named by the railroad workers who camped nearby, simply referring to the location as "Troutman's." It remained so named for years until the Richmond and Danville Railroad dropped the possessive and simply called it "Troutman." Another store responsible for growth in the village was Colonel J.M. Patterson's store, founded in 1870, which became well known for the local trade in rabbits, of which Patterson's shipped out literally thousands. Colonel Patterson also worked to move the old Fallstown Post Office to Troutman. It was moved near the railroad in 1866 and simply called Troutman Post Office. The town was incorporated in 1905 (population: 200).

Ostwalt's Mill, circa 1850, was a prosperous buhr mill destroyed by fire and then rebuilt in 1919, this time powered by electricity. In 1879, J.C. Steele, from the township of Cool Spring, operated a large sawmill lasting until 1889, when he moved to Statesville. The English Handle Works was established in Troutman by the Setzer brothers in 1890 and was one of the larger industries; for a decade, it made spokes and handles, hubs, wheel rims, shuttles, shuttle blocks for looms and tool handles, until the suitable young timber (the former "virgin forest") was depleted. However, growth in local manufacturing did not escalate until the introduction of electric power in 1919 by Troutman Power and Light, which organized to bring Southern Power lines from Barium Springs. Industry began to grow after World War I. Troutman Shirt Company and Troutman Chair were both organized in the 1920s and Raymer's Public Oil Company was organized in the 1930s.

The former Troutman train station, a small Late Victorian frame building, was moved to the Troutman Family Historical Grounds and restored. The Norwood School, circa 1906, is one of the ninety public schools built in the early twentieth century during the Aycock era. The most architecturally significant of the few schools still standing, it was also moved to the Troutman Family historical site and is now used as the family's historical building.

St. Michael's Lutheran Church was established in 1815 (some say 1812) two miles south of Troutman. St. Michael's was a log church that was destroyed by a fire. Rebuilt in the same location, it served from 1868 to 1886, when it was moved to Troutman, merging with the 1833 St. Martin's Church to become Holy Trinity Lutheran Church. St. James Episcopal Church in nearby Shinnville, in the township of Barringer, is one of the oldest congregations in the area (New Perth ARP, though it has no records, was formed before 1790, according to a Synod statement). St. James was built in 1856, a Gothic Revival church for the first Episcopal congregation in the county, and is the oldest Episcopal Church in Iredell in its original location. Remodeling has altered its appearance but many of its original furnishings are preserved. Another pre–Civil War church, Mount Carmel, was moved in 1894 to become Troutman Methodist Church.

The former Norwood School, circa 1906, now relocated to the Troutman Family Historical Grounds, Troutman. *Courtesy of the author.*

Bethel Baptist Church, near East Monbo, was established in 1860. See *Heritage of Iredell County* for more information.

Other Municipalities, Townships and Villages

As we rush to become a larger city, I hope we won't lose sight of our rural traditions and their pleasures.
—Rob Hites, Statesville City Manager, *2008* Record and Landmark, *Statesville*

In 1883, the Harmony Post Office was established near the 1846 Harmony Hill Camp Meeting Ground. The community in the township of Turnersburg became an academy town and a leading agricultural village and trading center in north Iredell. The name originates from the "harmony" meetings that were held there by a church group; a charming anecdote that cannot be proven by any record recounts that in an early meeting of village founders, a heated discussion arose over the naming of the village. To restore order, the presiding citizen banged his hand on the table and raised his voice, calling out, "Gentlemen, let us have harmony!" And, the rest, they say, is history. Harmony was incorporated in 1927 in order to acquire electric power from Duke Power Company and eventually overshadowed both Olin and Williamsburg.

The 1886 *Landmark* wrote, "While the township of Union Grove has no village or hamlet, it is probably as densely populated as any other township in the county." H.P. Van Hoy wrote that Union Grove got its name from the newly freed former slaves who would gather at an arbor they had built near a grove. This arbor stood as an emblem for the Union; therefore, they would gather at the "Union grove" for their meetings, eventually forming Union Grove Methodist Protestant Church. Other stories credit the concentration of Union sympathizers in the area during the Civil War to account for the name. An early subscription school, Douthit, was formed in 1830 and the Winthrop Friends, who had met in private homes since 1800, established the Winthrop Friends Meeting in 1890, the oldest in the county. A mill organized in 1934, the Union Grove Mill, was built to encourage Duke Power to extend its lines to the area.

East of Statesville, along the road to Mocksville, is the township of Cool Spring. A local legend claims that a Revolutionary War soldier stopped there for a drink of water and declared that it was indeed "a cool spring," having unusually cold water. A health spa was established in 1852 for patrons and travelers on the plank road nearby. After the Civil War, Cool Spring became an academy town—the Cool Spring Academy gave its name to the township, or vice versa, if one believes the Revolutionary War story. Hollingswood, a Georgian Colonial plantation house, circa 1850, served as home for the teachers at the nearby academy. It is almost completely original and well preserved. The 1846 Fifth Creek Presbyterian Church is also a landmark. One of the last operating cotton gins is located in the area, operating until 1976 (Cool Spring was once a large producer of cotton).

Hollingswood Plantation, circa 1850–1860, Greek Revival, also known as Vaughn's Mill Place, is in Cool Spring Township. *Courtesy of the author.*

Fifth Creek Presbyterian Church, established 1846, is now a country Gothic Revival–style building circa 1890, Cool Spring Township. *Courtesy of the author.*

Another early spa was attempted at Powder Springs (named for its water, which tasted like gunpowder), later renamed Eupeptic ("good digestion") Springs. Located in north Iredell, Eupeptic Springs did not last as a spa and the resort area was sold after three years as the idea of "healing water" passed. A spa was also attempted at Barium Springs, when a Mooresville businessman purchased one hundred acres of the Linster Farm in 1885, acquiring the eight natural springs on the property. Called Poison Springs by the Indians, whose animals would not drink the water, the 1886 hotel at Poison Springs was purchased in 1889 and the rather unlovely name was changed to Barium Springs. The hotel burned and the unsuccessful spa was sold to the Presbyterian Synod who moved their small orphanage in Charlotte to the site. The early buildings are gone but the Lottie Walker Women's Building, circa 1922, and the Burrough's Office Building, circa 1908, remain as two of the older buildings on the campus. A remnant of the healing spring can still be found on the site.

The village of East Monbo, in the Fallstown Township, existed because of C.L. Turner's two mills, one on each side of the Catawba River. A concrete dam spanned the river between the cotton mill on the Catawba side of the river, and the yarn mill (built in 1907) on the Iredell side of the river. The Monbo Manufacturing Company provided for the occupants of the village's forty-two mill houses and a company store. The name was originally Mont Beau (beautiful mountain), but it was slurred over the years and became "Monbo." In 1910, the mills were reorganized as Turner Mills Co. and the Iredell side mill was opened to produce yarn. After the flood of 1916, the Turner Mills Co. suffered

The 1922 Neoclassical Revival Lottie Walker Building at Barium Springs Home for Children, near Troutman. *Courtesy of the author.*

Freedom United Presbyterian Church, established 1865, was the first African American congregation established after the Civil War, and one of the earliest African American congregations in the Western Piedmont. *Courtesy of the author.*

the devastating destruction of the Catawba mill, but the Iredell mill was only flooded on the ground floor and continued operations as Superior Yarn Mill until 1960, when the Cowan's Ford Dam was built.

The 1888 *Landmark* wrote, "In Bethany-township there is not a store, a grist mill, a saw mill, or a post office. It is the only township in the county without a post office and the only one which is without one of the other things mentioned." But Bethany is one of the larger townships with Bethany Church, organized in 1775, and the landmark Ebenezer School. Other early schools included Hampton, Fairview, Duffy's, Moore's, Bethany, Haywood and Morrison's. The first African American congregation established Freedom United Presbyterian Church in 1865 in Bethany, and it was one of the first churches for African Americans in the western Piedmont. John Nisbet operated the first store between Salisbury and Wilkesboro at Bethany, until his 1788 move to the Statesville town square.

The founding of Love Valley has clearly been the most ambitious and unique experiment in the county. Andy Barker built an "authentic" western town in the foothills of the Brushy Mountains in the township of New Hope. The town, modeled after a stereotypical nineteenth-century village (albeit a western village), has a rustic saloon and general store, and is replete with a western feel, down to the "hitching post" on the street. It was built in 1954 with its own post office, which is the only new rural system set up since the advent of rural free delivery nearly a half century before the town's inception. In 1956, the Presbyterian Church was organized in the little town. Mr. Barker founded the Southeastern Rodeo Association in 1956, and in 1959, he incorporated the Chickasaw Horse Association. The town itself was incorporated in 1963 (population: sixty). Two rodeos are held annually and the Love Valley Stables are located there. As Faulkner said, "The past is never dead. It is not even past." And that is so true in Love Valley. The past is alive again, in a town that is an ongoing experiment in living history! For more information about Love Valley, see *Love Valley, An American Utopia*, by Conrad Ostwalt.

Heritage of Iredell County, Vol. I contains several articles discussing the small towns and villages that flourished in Iredell County. For more information, see "Liberty Hill" by Mildred Miller, "Stony Point" by W.N. Watt, "Eagle Mills" by Mildred Miller, "Turnersburg" by Dorothy Summerville, "Union Grove" by Jennings and Adams, "Williamsburg" by Victor Crosby and Articles 41, 42, 44, 51 and 54. Vol. II includes "New Hope, Jennings, and Union Grove" by Mike Trivette and Article 135.

Statesville's Emerging Markets

The old favorite, the Meyer-Thorne Comedy Company, will play a three night engagement at Opera Hall beginning Monday night next with "A Woman's Devotion." Popular prices 35 & 50 cents. Tickets are on sale at Messers. Clark and Meyer.

–1887 Landmark

The *Iredell Express* revived after Stoneman's raid, becoming the *Statesville American*, 1865–1886, published by Eugene Drake. The *Statesville Intelligencer*, established in 1872, was lost in 1874 when the publisher bought the old *Charlotte Observer* and moved (there are a few issues on microfilm at Mitchell College). In June of 1874, the *Landmark*, a conservative paper, was established. In 1892, when it was sold, the printing department was sold to John A. Brady. Both operated for years on the second floor of the future Holmes Drug Store on the square (in 1906, Brady Printing relocated and again in 1957, moving to its current location on Salisbury Road). By 1918, the *Landmark* published twice a week, and nearly complete files are on microfilm at the offices of the *Record and Landmark* on East Broad Street. The *Mascot* published briefly and the *Sentinel* appeared in 1893 and lasted until the mid-1920s. The *Piedmont Sun*, a paper focused on the African American community, was a Statesville weekly from 1896 to 1898, but no copies are known to survive. (See *Heritage of Iredell County*, Vol. I.)

All of the water-powered mills in the northern part of the county had been successful but with the failure of the proposed Airline Railroad, the north remained primarily rural and most of the mills died. Tobacco, whiskey, cotton and furniture manufacture began to replace the devastated agricultural economy and the tobacco and cotton trades were greatly expanded. Grain, corn and distilled liquors, as well as tobacco and cotton, were shipped out of Iredell with cotton surpassing herbs and produce as a cash crop. The

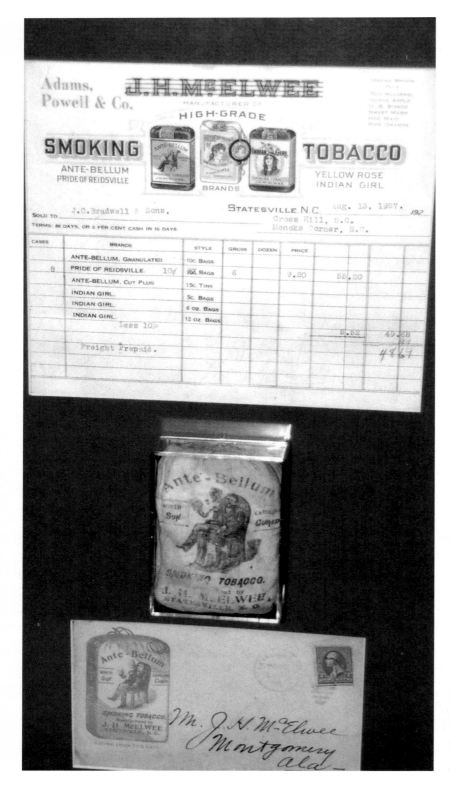

McElwee
Tobacco
memorabilia.
*Courtesy of the
Statesville Historical
Collection of Dr.
Steve Hill.*

1882 *Landmark* stated that the first gin in North Carolina was made and operated in Iredell County. But tobacco continued to be a popular crop and Dr. Steve Hill's private collection of Statesville memorabilia contains over one hundred tobacco products manufactured locally including cigars, smoking tobacco, plugs and twists from eighteen different brands. In the 1880s and 1890s, Iredell had four tobacco factories and two cigar-makers, producing fifty-five brands of chewing tobacco and six brands of smoking tobacco. The best-known brand was McElwee's "Indian Girl" smoking tobacco.

The spread of the railroad (all railroads had been incorporated into Southern Railways system by 1894) supplanted Statesville's monopoly on trade, with other markets in new towns, and in 1882 alone, over one thousand bushels of wheat were grown within the town limits of Mooresville and over eighty thousand bushels were grown in greater Iredell. North Iredell had over twenty thousand acres under cultivation by 1900, and threshing machines were in use and portable. Separators were common by the end of the nineteenth century, as well as binding machines to take the place of hand cutting and binding. (By the end of the Civil War, mowing machines, sulky rakes, circular saws, cookstoves and sewing machines were also common.) Even with the new mechanical innovations, farmers were not as prosperous as the town-dwelling wholesalers and merchants. Large row crops, relying on a sizeable and seasonal labor force, could not be mechanized. This resulted in the development of sharecropping; by 1880, nearly one-fourth of all tenants were sharecroppers, many of whom were former slaves who had chosen to remain on farms. To represent farmers' interests, the Grange and other agricultural associations were formed.

A 1910 photograph of McElwee Tobacco Warehouse clients waiting on Water Street in Statesville.
Courtesy of the Greater Statesville Chamber of Commerce

85

The former McElwee Tobacco Factory in the late nineteenth century, near the Statesville Depot. By 1918, the site was a hotel. *Courtesy of the author.*

By 1880, Statesville was the center of the distilling industry with government-licensed distilleries throughout the county. That same year, the AT&O shipped fifty-seven thousand gallons of liquor from Iredell over a six-month period. The 1884 *Landmark* lists four liquor wholesalers in Statesville, with one shipping out three thousand gallons of apple brandy in one day. The 1897 *Landmark* lists twenty-six grain distilleries and twenty-one fruit distilleries in the county.

Leather continued to be made and processed. Lumbering was still a very big industry, and nearly every grinding mill had a sawmill attached. The structure that dominated the skyline was the Statesville Flour Mill, established in 1892. It was built on the site of the old Spoke and Handle Works and Wagner's Barrel Factory. The mill was destroyed by fire in 1908 but was rebuilt that same year. It still stands as a landmark in Statesville and is operated by Bartlett Milling.

In 1870, there were six small brickyards in Statesville, from which one major brick company emerged. J.C. Steele and Sons, a leading manufacturer of clay-working machinery, is another nineteenth-century business that is still a town landmark, beginning its life as the New South Brickworks in 1889. J.C. Steele took over the Sword Brick Making Machine and the foundry of a 1887 plow factory to make bricks for the Hotel Iredell, the twenty-six-room, three-story hotel that once stood across from the Old Courthouse. The company has been run by four generations of the Steele family and the original building is a working part of the complex on South Mulberry Street. Steele, from Cool Spring, was mayor of the town at one time and facilitated the

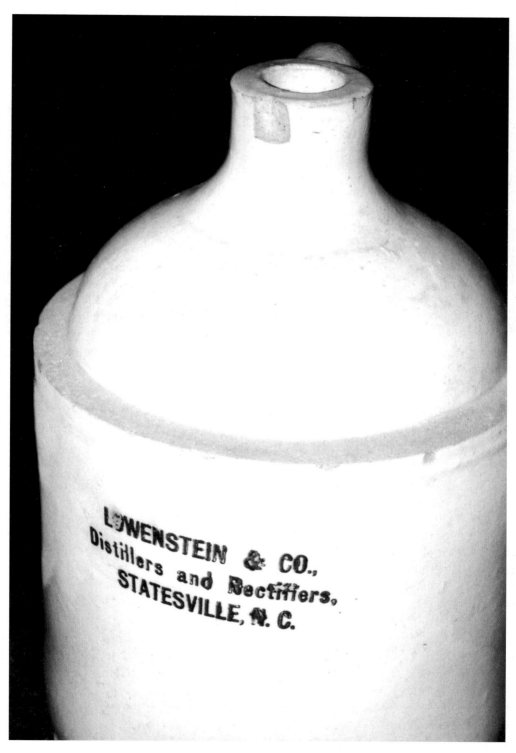

Lowenstein & Co. whiskey jug. *Courtesy of Iredell Museums.*

The 1892 Statesville Flour Mill, now Bartlett Milling. The long, brick, four-story building in the center is an original building. *Courtesy of the author.*

J.C. Steele & Sons on South Mulberry Street, Statesville. The rear wing is an original building from circa 1889. *Courtesy of the author.*

acquisition of the cannon and cannonballs on the lawn of the Old Courthouse, placed there in 1905. (The cannons are still in place but the two pyramids of cannonballs are nowhere to be found!)

Isaac and David Wallace had opened a general store in 1859, beginning their wholesale business in 1866, trading manufactured goods for produce. Later, their herbarium became the largest business of its type in the United States; by 1890, they had shipped over a million pounds of herbal products covering over two thousand varieties of plants. The herbarium was located at Walnut and Meeting Streets but was torn down in 1944. An expansion building built by Isidore Wallace still stands on Meeting Street, south of Armfield (it was sold as a furniture warehouse in 1912). *The Inventory of Historic Architecture* credits this building to Wallace; however, *Iredell County Landmarks* credits the building to R.V. Brawley and L. Pinkus, who operated a herbarium as well. The 1882 *Landmark* wrote,

> *The oldest and largest business is Wallace Brothers, exclusive wholesale dealers in merchandise with three stores on Broad and an immense Herbarium, largest in the world. The largest retail stock in town is Irvin and Company, which has some of everything. Hoffman Brothers established the first fancy grocery store in town. To fancy is added heavy groceries, fruits, and confections.*

An expansion building of the Wallace Brothers Herbarium, built by Isidore Wallace (or the Brawley Pinkus Herbarium—sources conflict for this site). *Courtesy of the author.*

By 1883, Statesville had kerosene streetlamps monitored by a village "lamplighter" and there were rail fences along the streets in the residential area. The few sidewalks in town were plank and public wells sat in the middle of the wide streets. Some city residents had electric lights in 1888; by 1890, a steam-driven plant on Water Street provided electric lights for the town, with carbon arc lamps on the downtown streets. The first public water system opened in 1899. A boiler and steam pump pushed water up to a cistern at the college, at that time called Statesville Female College, the highest spot in town. (The old pumping station is still standing.) The 1876 volunteer hook and ladder company, pumping water from underground cisterns, had graduated from six buckets in 1869 to a fire department in 1875, adding a steam LaFrance fire engine by 1882. In 1899, the fire company was organized as Statesville Reel Co. No. 1. The first gasoline-driven truck was purchased in 1912, but the horse-drawn fire wagon lasted until 1918 before being replaced by a second motor-driven engine.

The 1885 *Landmark* stated, "One of the greatest nuisances to which this town is subjected is the ringing of the court house bell at all sorts of hours for all sorts of purposes." In 1899, a contract was made for the building of a new courthouse, Statesville's fourth. The *Landmark* reported, "The building of a new court house threw consternation into the occupants when it was torn down…The Idle Hour Club, who won't whittle and yarn the hours away under the shadows of the tall granite pillars, were disconsolate."

The 1910 Statesville Fire Department. *Courtesy of the Greater Statesville Chamber of Commerce.*

(No mention was made of a new courthouse bell.) This new landmark is today called the Old Courthouse, on the corner of Court and Center Streets. The Beaux-Arts–style building, on the National Register, is home to county and administrative offices. The old jail on East Broad Street served until 1873, when a new jail was built behind the new courthouse on South Center Street. In the early 1900s, this jail was replaced by a "new and elegant jail of modern construction." This new jail is a fortress-like building of yellow brick. It still stands and is now the "Old Jail" behind the "Old Courthouse" and home to the Iredell Arts Council. See www.iredellarts.org.

There were two banks established near the end of the nineteenth century—the First Building and Loan, circa 1887, and the First National Bank on the square, which existed until 1933. The 1899 *Landmark* reported that, "First National has bought the vacant corner at East Broad and South Center Streets, vacant from the 1882 fire when it had been the site of the old Bell Store Warehouse." This corner building is now generally known as the "clock tower." Statesville had wanted a town clock since the 1854 fire; by 1890, a town clock topped the First National Bank Building. The clock chimed the hour until World War II, when the bell was donated for scrap metal for the war effort. A new, smaller chime was installed and then replaced by a recorded alarm that notified volunteers of any local fires. (Neither has been heard in quite a long while.) Both the First National Building and the clock tower are now preserved under private ownership. The roofline has changed via the addition of a brick apron to replace the decorative iron and pressed-tin parapet that was dangerously deteriorated by the twentieth century and

The 1899 Iredell County Courthouse in Statesville, with its unique, tiled mansard roof, is now known as the "Old Courthouse." *Courtesy of the author.*

A drawing of the Old Courthouse, Statesville's fourth. *Courtesy of Iredell Museums.*

The old jail, circa 1910, in Statesville. *Courtesy of the Greater Statesville Chamber of Commerce.*

beginning to threaten pedestrians on the street below. (In the 1950s, local photographer Max Tharpe noted that the hour of eleven on one of the clock faces actually read "XII" not "XI;" that, at least, was corrected. But, what did happen to our bell?). The 1897 *Landmark* reported:

> *The First National Bank has in use quite a unique and convenient counting machine. It is called the Burroughs Registering Accountant, and registers any amount, from one cent to one thousand dollars. The figures are on the top of the machine like a typewriter and all you have to do is press the figures, turn the crank, and the amount is registered plainly on a slip of paper.*

After the Civil War, over forty post offices were put on "star routes" all over the county, but most of these were discontinued in the early 1900s with the advent of free rural mail delivery service, which was accomplished over only seventeen routes with a horse and buggy. For details on all of the early post offices, see Homer Keever's *Iredell, Piedmont County* and Mildred Miller's listing of late nineteenth-century post offices from the National Archives in Washington, D.C., reprinted in *Heritage of Iredell County*, Vol. I. In 1892, Statesville's new post office was built by the Federal government and free city delivery began in 1902. The new building, at Center and Front Streets, was to be a two-story brownstone building but its realization was slightly different from the government plans. "Old City Hall" is listed on the National Register and its style is described as Richardsonian Romanesque. The warm red-brick building with slightly medieval features is a unique accent to the architecture of downtown Statesville. It was used as the Statesville Post Office and Federal Court building for fifty years. The county government took over the use of the building known as "Old City Hall" in 1939, when the new post office and courthouse opened at Broad and Meeting Streets. The new building is no longer a post office but is still home to the courts.

The telephone also began in the late nineteenth century, having been invented in 1876. In 1894, an exclusive franchise was granted to the city council for the Statesville Telephone Company and the first exchange opened the next year with forty-eight subscribers. Southern Bell Telephone established long-distance calling in 1898. Several independent rural exchanges operated as Iredell Telephone, an organization of small exchanges in the county, from 1898 to 1901. Southern Bell bought the Statesville Telephone franchise in 1906 after what are politely called the "franchise wars." The result was a local carrier, Iredell, and a long-distance carrier, Southern Bell, who eventually won the franchise debacle to become the sole carrier by 1906. It would be 1949 before a central board and operators were replaced with manual dialing and well into the latter twentieth century before multiparty lines were eliminated. The Postal Telegraph also operated in Statesville from 1908 to 1943.

Local doctors establishing their practices in the area included: B.F. Douglas at Liberty Hill; T.C. Halyburton at Stony Point; R.W. Mills in Troutman; and S.E. Evans and Thomas Anderson in Statesville. Dr. John F. Long partnered with Dr. Robert Campbell, beginning their practice in Statesville after the Civil War and performing the first

The 1892 Statesville Post Office, known as Old City Hall since 1939. Image from a 1910 photograph. *Courtesy of the Greater Statesville Chamber of Commerce.*

Original Treasury Department plans for the Statesville Post Office, circa 1892. *Courtesy of Iredell Museums.*

Long's Sanatorium, circa 1905, with Dr. H.F. Long's home pictured on the left. *Courtesy of the Greater Statesville Chamber of Commerce.*

surgery, a leg amputation. Long was joined by his son, Dr. Henry F. Long, in 1893. In 1896, after an appendectomy was performed on a kitchen table, Dr. H.F. Long invented a collapsible, portable operating table. In 1897, Long opened a small temporary hospital in a room in the Hotel Iredell, then in a private home. Long's Sanatorium, circa 1905 (later the H.F. Long Hospital, circa 1933), established by Dr. Long on North Center Street, was the first privately owned hospital in the state. His home and the hospital are still standing, the former hospital used as the Iredell County Building Standards Center. For a history of African American doctors in the community, see Phyllis Bailey's work in *Iredell County Tracks*, Vol. XXVII, No. 2.

In the 1880s, there were many new churches built by established congregations at new locations. In Statesville, the First Associate Reformed Presbyterian Church on East Broad Street remains at its original location (circa 1892) and the First Presbyterian Church remains on the site of the 1750s Fourth Creek Meeting House. The final major denomination to establish itself was the Lutheran Church—St. John's Lutheran Church, which had met on the upper floor of a music store in 1888, built a church at Front and Mulberry Streets in 1891. It is now Holsey Memorial CME Church. The Key Memorial, St. Philip Apostle Church (later St. Pius X), was built in 1918 in honor of Philip Barton Key. This small Gothic Revival church is now the home of the popular weekly tabloid, the *Iredell Citizen*. Temple Emanuel is the second-oldest synagogue in North Carolina and the second-oldest house of worship in Statesville, built in 1891 at the boundary of the old Fourth Creek Burying Ground at North Kelly Street and West End Avenue. Listed on the National Register, it is a mixture of Romanesque Revival and Gothic styles, with an unchanged interior that includes a rare fresco. It was also the first building built with an eye toward future electric lighting. The oldest house of worship in Statesville was built as

The 1891 St. John's Lutheran Church, now Holsey Memorial CME Church, Statesville. *Courtesy of the author.*

Temple Emanuel, circa 1891, is the second-oldest house of worship in Statesville. *Courtesy of the author.*

the Chapel of the Cross in 1876 by the Trinity Episcopal congregation, and it has been the Friends Meeting House on Walnut Street since the 1960s.

Indeed, the thirty-five years after the heartbreaking losses of the Civil War seemed full of progress, but the country suffered a major slowdown in the economy at the end of the nineteenth century. The business decline of the early 1890s was a low point in the business cycle, common in industrial economies. It was worse than the turn of the nineteenth or mid-nineteenth centuries but not as devastating as the Great Depression. Political conflict erupted with a Populist "rebellion" that attempted to make the economy, rather than race, a primary issue. Populists did not upset the system, but from the debate came a New South ideology focused on economic development, segregated but peaceful race relations (even though the Jim Crow laws were put into effect in 1899 and negated most of the gains of Reconstruction) and improved educational systems with public graded schools from circa 1891. The last decade of the nineteenth century also focused on three major issues locally—the construction of an electric power station, the graded school system and the construction of a water and sewer system.

The Statesville Board of Education was established in 1885 (Iredell Board of Education circa 1897) and, in 1891, Statesville voted a tax for the graded schools with a dual system to separate the races. (The 1868 North Carolina Constitution had provided for public education four months a year. The 1869 constitution had provided for segregation.) In 1893, white students went to an academy on Bell Street also called the South School (later changed to Mulberry Street School). African American students went to a school on Green Street, which later became Morningside Graded School.

The 1876 Chapel of the Cross, built by the Trinity Episcopal Church congregation, is the oldest house of worship in Statesville, and since the 1960s has been the Friends Meeting House. *Courtesy of the author.*

The Hotel Iredell on its former South Center Street site. *Courtesy of the Statesville Historical Collection of Dr. Steve Hill.*

The Statesville town clock "on the square," circa 1910. *Courtesy of the Statesville Historical Collection of Dr. Steve Hill.*

The 1897 Hotel Iredell in the foreground, located on South Center Street, Statesville. *Courtesy of the Greater Statesville Chamber of Commerce.*

Mitchell College had been sold to the Davidson College Board of Trustees and then to Robert and Roxanne Simonton, who changed the name to Simonton Female College. They also chose two administrators who would have a lasting effect on the college. Elizabeth Mitchell Grant and her sister Margaret Mitchell assumed the helm of the college, their eventual namesake, in 1875. The Simonton Female College was sold to a group of Statesville businessmen but the depression in the spring of 1893 resulted in the college closing for three years. Upon its reopening, the college was again attached to the Concord Presbytery and called Statesville Female College.

The town no longer has its old hotels. The Commercial House, later the Chandler House Hotel (circa 1855), is gone. The favored hotel—the 1897 Hotel Iredell—that had previously been the Cooper House Hotel, built in 1885, burned down in 1918. The St. Charles Hotel, previously an old tavern, was torn down in 1955. But at the turn of the twentieth century, Statesville had her hotels and a wonderful Victorian "picture postcard" atmosphere. A new depot was built in 1911 and buggies carried passengers from the depot to the hotels. On the main street there were specialty shops, milliners, an ice cream saloon, three drugstores with soda fountains, two jewelers dealing mostly in clocks and three music stores selling pianos and organs. The first clothing house was M. Stein & Sons, of Baltimore. The first slot machine in town was installed in 1890, dispensing nickel cigars. The furniture store sold coffins as well as furnishings and case goods. There were also the requisite grocers, butchers and farm supply stores. And there were still dances, programs and concerts held at the Opera Hall in the Stockton Building

PROGRAM

⊱ЕЗ⊰

Introducing as **MISTRESS OF CEREMONIES**:   MISS MILDRED SHERRILL

Overtures—"HITS OF TODAY,"   -   -   The Davidsonian's Orchestra

Opening Song—"HERE COMES THE SHOW BOAT"
. Cowles Bristol and Entire Company

Introducing as Guests of Show Boat:

Misses Elizabeth Holland, Beulah Henley, Robbin Fraley, Lula Furches, Louise Moroney, Fannie Gilliam, Susie Greenwood, Estelle Reddick.

Messrs. Bill Pipkins, Clarence Johnson, Jack Sentman, John Boyd, Tommie Lee Kincaid, Fred Poston, Bill Fisher, Jack Joyner, Earl Jones, Jimmie Goode.

ACT I.

Dr. Frank White's "HEE-HAW BITTERS" MEDICINE SHOW,
Introducing the following characters:

Dr. Frank White,   -   -   -   -   -   Murray Grier
His Comedians: Ed. Daniels, J. B. Abernathy, Sam Hall, Bill Fisher

ACT II.

Gastonia's Favorite Male Quartet: "SOUTHLAND'S SWEETEST SINGERS"

| JOE OVERMEYER | ROGER GRIER |
| PERK THOMPSON | HUB GLENN |

Mrs. HUGH A. QUERY, Accompanist

ACT III.

MISS ELIZABETH PRESSLY,   -   -   -   -   -   Recitation

ACT IV.

Double Sextette—SONG AND DANCE OFFERING:

"LET US SWEAR IT BY THE PALE MOONLIGHT"

Misses Beth Sloop, Margaret Adams, Mary Guerrant, Dot Tomlin Helen Brawley, Margaret Abernathy.

Messrs. Karl Deaton, Bob Collier, John Long, Allen Knox, Jac Sentman, Dewey Raymer.

Assisted by Margaret Pennington, and Allen Knox.

Turn-of-the-twentieth-century public entertainment program. *Courtesy of Iredell Museums.*

Nineteenth-century poster advertising clothing. *Courtesy of the Statesville Historical Collection of Dr Steve Hill.*

as well as minstrel shows, singers, bands, skating, dramas, receptions, teas, large picnics, straw rides, piano concerts, literary clubs, spelling bees, debating, circuses, hunting, fishing and quail and turkey shoots. And of course, there was baseball beginning in 1875, with football following in 1889 and basketball in 1907. Movie theaters arrived just before World War I and changed our idea of entertainment forever.

Chapter 4

The Twentieth Century

Great Changes for the Towns, Villages and Townships of Iredell County

Good Roads

A piece of true macadam, the first in town, was done on Center Street, from the public well to north of the Landmark *office.*

—1885 Landmark

The twentieth-century South was plagued with tumultuous emotions and ill-considered class and color conflict, as well as awkward attempts to change the "Southern system." Reconstruction remained slow and painful, and was rife with contradiction. Even so, this milieu of old beliefs and progressive ideas—new inventions and the comfort of the familiar—resulted in a progressive period in government and education during the 1900s, with inherited social, economic and political structures left in question.

The economy had shifted from trading to manufacturing in both Statesville and Mooresville, with cotton mills dominating early manufacturing enterprises. The dam at Lookout Shoals began to produce electricity at the hydroelectric plant and the switch from steam engines to electric power was complete by 1915. Electricity and the telephone ended the onus of small-town isolation but good roads and the automobile would prove to be the catalyst for even greater change, soon becoming indispensable.

The "good roads" movement, in Mooresville, began in 1910. The slogan of the Mooresville "good roads" boosters was "The Best Way to Anywhere is by Mooresville!" As early as 1903, the first mile of good road in Iredell was built out of Mooresville, but by 1911, there were still only eight miles of improved roads in south Iredell and sixteen miles in north Iredell. That same year, a central highway was routed from Salisbury to Asheville, splitting the route between Mooresville and Statesville. In 1913, the Post Road from Winston-Salem to Statesville would mirror the route of Interstate 40 today, and by early 1914, Iredell had 230 miles of improved roads. But, for rural areas, macadam paving was not done, and by 1913, sand-clay roads were the norm in the county. Rural roads only began to improve in the 1930s as the state took over road improvement projects.

The last livery stable in Statesville was gone by 1918 and the horse and buggy had virtually disappeared by 1920 with the popularization of the automobile. There were

Mooresville "good roads" boosters, circa 1910. *Courtesy Mooresville Historical Society.*

eight cars in Statesville in 1908, but these numbers grew exponentially. In 1910, Webb Fox opened the first dealership next to the Henkel Stables on North Center Street. In 1912, Carolina Motor Company was one of the fifty original Ford dealers in the United States and the first Ford dealership in North Carolina. Their building on East Broad Street is much the same now and is the home of a local school. The Yount building on West Broad Street was also the site of an early car dealership selling Maxwells, the forebear of Chrysler. (Gene Krider, a local historian, relates that the first girls' basketball team once played their games on the second-floor car storage at this site, which was also used for dances at one time.) The speed limit was six miles per hour in town and fifteen miles per hour elsewhere.

Statesville's Merchants and Farmers

All these things are gone now-tobacco manufacture, the herb and cotton industries, and the wholesale liquor trade.

—Homer Keever, 1976

The ebullient market town of Statesville was no longer a wholesale trade center, the last vestiges of which disappeared completely after World War I. North Carolina enacted statewide prohibition in 1909 and was one of the first states to do so. The Temperance

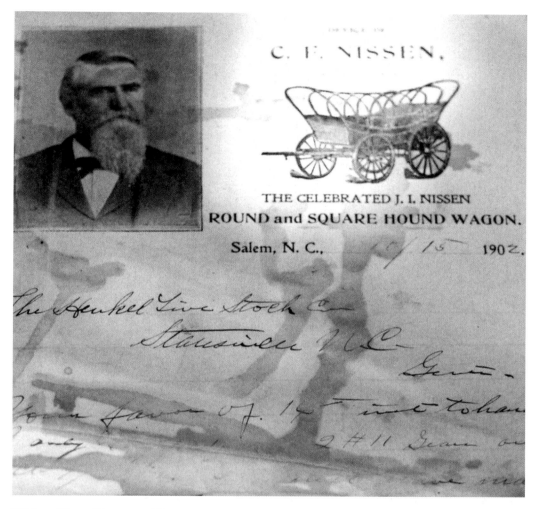

Bill from Nissen Wagon, established in the eighteenth century in Salem (Winston-Salem), sent to Henkel Livestock Co., Statesville. *Courtesy of Iredell Museums.*

Society was entrenched, having begun in 1833 in Statesville as an alarmed response to the growing liquor industry. The Society petitioned, picketed and even marched, hatchets in hands, to the depot to chop up barrels of whiskey awaiting shipment. The 1886 *Landmark* reported that, "The temperance movement is enjoying quite a boom…[although] one lady in town has declined to sign because she is not willing to give up her sweet elder in summertime!" In 1891, another *Landmark* story featured news of a local wagon wreck that resulted in a stream of corn liquor bursting out of the kegs, from which "some residents of the neighborhood drank copiously." In 1903, "local option" prohibition effectively suffocated the industry in Iredell.

The primary grocery wholesaler in 1900 was gone by mid-century, as were many country stores. The community stores remaining today are few. Mike Trivette and Hal

A Nissen wagon, one of only three remaining Nissen wagons in North Carolina. *Courtesy of Iredell Museums.*

A Plymouth dealership on North Center Street, Statesville, in the 1950s. *Courtesy of the Statesville Historical Collection of Dr. Steve Hill.*

The old Belk Department Store on South Center Street, Statesville. *Courtesy of the Statesville Historical Collection of Dr. Steve Hill.*

Henderson have compiled pictures and stories of these stores in *Heritage of Iredell County*, Vol. II, featuring the once-numerous country and community stores. The Jennings Store, circa 1857, in the Jennings community, is a crossroads general store complex that has run continuously except for a few years in the late 1970s. Today, the store features arts and crafts made locally and is operated by a fifth-generation descendant of founder T.L. Jennings. Next door, the 1889 Neoclassical Revival farmhouse, remodeled in 1910, is the residence of family members. There is also an apple warehouse on the property, now used as alternate living quarters. The store is a pleasant step back in time and is situated in the beautiful countryside near Union Grove. Jennings Store was featured in the *Iredell Citizen* of October 23, 2003.

Many small nineteenth-century local specialty shops were also closed, sold or absorbed by larger stores, until the chain store phenomenon took root much later in the century and denuded many small-town main streets. The oldest commercial site in Statesville was once the Marble Hall Saloon with its rather grand Georgia-marble floor and bar, built in one of the town's oldest buildings at 115 South Center Street. It was the location of Statesville Drug in 1904, which moved to the square into the former location of the First National Bank (in the clock tower) in 1937. The doctors' offices that were on the second floor of the building, and the drugstore, are gone now. Noted local historian, Dr. P.F. Laugenour (also a dentist), had his office there, along with others whose names are still stenciled on the half-glass interior doors and

Lois Jennings behind the counter at the Jennings General Store near Union Grove. *Courtesy of Mr. David Hicks.*

A 1910 photograph of the shops on Broad Street, Statesville. *Courtesy of the Greater Statesville Chamber of Commerce.*

second-story exterior windows. Another of the oldest "brick and iron" buildings in Statesville, across the square from the clock tower, was originally a private home and then a grocery, a mercantile establishment and two different drugstores until 1932; in that year, Ralph Holmes bought the property and it continued as Holmes Drug Store for many years. It is now the site of La Dolce Vita Café.

Although the first hardware store in town was the 1858 Cole Hardware at 109 East Broad Street, Lazenby-Montgomery Hardware Store, established in 1905, remains today as a historic landmark. It had been W.A. Thomas and Company in 1894, but around the turn of the century Mr. Lazenby and Mr. Montgomery went to work there, astutely buying the store, which continued until the 1980s. The building is now the home of the Frame Gallery on West Broad Street. The 1934 façade has been restored and the interior, with its balcony that was designed for greater hardware display, is intact. Michael Joe Moore currently exhibits his watercolors of historic Statesville in the gallery.

Nu Way Shoe Shop on East Broad Street, behind the clock tower building, was established in 1923. The shop is still open eighty-five years later, with its original wooden floors and wonderful smells of leather and polishes. It is run by the third generation of the Cornacchione family and is featured in Mike Lassiter's *Our Vanishing Americana*. Gene Krider, a living library of local lore, tells of watching the bottling of Coca-Cola through the large front windows of the former Coca-Cola Hall near the corner of Front and Meeting Streets. The rear upper floor of the split-level building was used

One of the older downtown buildings in Statesville, for many years the home of Holmes Drug Store on "the square," and now the home of La Dolce Vita Café. *Courtesy of the author.*

The former site of the Lazenby Montgomery Hardware Store in Statesville (circa 1905), now the Frame Gallery. *Courtesy of the author.*

for entertainment and dances and for variety shows by the Barium Springs orphans for fundraising. The Coca-Cola Hall, free to townspeople, was once an early car dealership as well, and is now the site of Rosenfeld CPA offices. Another important landmark is the 1921 Vance Hotel, listed on the National Register, and appropriately located on Front and Center Streets.

The 1907–1908 Statesville *City Directory* lists three banks, fourteen manufacturing concerns, four grocers, two newspapers, thirteen offices and shops, three druggists, four dentists, one veterinarian, three hotels, four schools, fifteen attorneys, five nurses and ten doctors. Gary Freeze, in *The Inventory of Historic Architecture*, writes: "Statesville has enviable historical architectural resources…few towns in North Carolina can claim the survival of such a large percentage of Victorian buildings." Freeze adds that the four axial streets forming the square are "blocks of quaint old brick stores and historic government buildings."

Rise of the Factory Worker

Statesville has everything but a coffin factory!

–Homer Keever, 1976

The major local differences between the last half of the nineteenth century and the early twentieth century were the increasing number of factory workers and a local economy based on manufacturing rather than trade. Mooresville had easy access to the railroad and to the large cotton fields in south Iredell and began to focus on cotton mills. Mooresville Cotton Mills, organized in 1893, was the first mechanized industry in the town, opening in 1894 (it was sold to Burlington in 1955). Dixie Cotton Mills, organized in 1906 producing yarn, was reorganized as Cascade Mills in 1923 (Cascade closed from 1929 to 1934 and was then also acquired by Burlington Industries). Textiles formed the engine moving the economy in Mooresville and the town became the second-largest manufacturer of towels in the world. The first textile mill in Statesville was the 1894 Statesville Cotton Mills, run by steam. Noble Bloomfield Mills opened Bloomfield Cotton Mill, the second oldest textile mill. Paola Cotton Mills in the west-side industrial area opened in 1907. Paola Yarn still operates today in the same location and is the least altered of all the industrial sites in town.

Statesville Furniture, established in 1901, was the first major furniture manufacturer. Others soon followed, and there was growth in the veneer industry in answer to growing demand in the marketplace after World War I. Louis Gordon founded Gordon Furniture in 1917, moving to its longtime location on North Center Street, the site of a former chair factory, in 1920. Gordon Scrap Metal, which was located behind the furniture store, moved to the Belmont Underpass in 1949 and is still a major industrial concern in Statesville. Statesville Brick was established in 1909 as Buffalo Clay Company, which consolidated as Statesville Brick in 1920. The company, located outside Statesville, is still a premier brickworks. In 1910, Morrison and Sons established Star Milling in Bloomfield. It

The 1921 Vance Hotel is still a Statesville landmark. *Courtesy of the author.*

Shops on South Center Street circa 1910. *Courtesy of the Statesville Historical Collection of Dr. Steve Hill.*

Former Mooresville mill owner's home. *Courtesy of the author.*

is now owned and operated by the Cashion family at its original location. Sherrill Lumber was established in 1916, the oldest firm of its kind in the area, and is now the site of Smith Phillips Building Supply; Slane Glass Company was established in 1906.

Needlework factories also existed before the Depression, the largest being the McNeer Dillon Company, which began the manufacture of sports and infant's wear in 1919; in 1957 it moved to the site of the unfinished Barnes Hotel at Walnut and Meeting Streets, now the Plaza Apartments.

Other industries of note in the area included the Rocky Creek Mill, which began its life in the nineteenth century as the Turner Mill; it was bought by C.V. Henkel and operated as the Henkel Mill until 1955 (Rocky Creek Mill was eventually bought by J.P. Stevens). Hubbard Farms was organized in 1921; the Bunch Hatchery, the South's oldest and largest hatchery, began operations in 1926. Phoenix Mills began operations in 1927 (it was later purchased by Beaunit). Gilbert Engineering was organized in 1928.

Between 1929 and 1932, the Great Depression, with its devastating weight of economic problems and unemployment, impacted the South, causing crisis upon crisis and disruption in commerce and industry. Workers protested wages and conditions. Mills closed. Banks failed. Locally, there was very little industrial expansion and residential development; however, Stimpson Hoisery Mills opened in Statesville around 1930, and the company of Ervin-West Construction was established that same year (in 1939, the name Ervin-West was changed to P.S. West Construction, as we know it today).

The Turner Yarn Mill (early twentieth century) on the Catawba River at East Monbo. *Courtesy of Iredell Museums.*

Millworkers at the Turner Mill at East Monbo in the early twentieth century. *Courtesy of Iredell Museums.*

J.T. Alexander and Sons opened in 1935 and is now operated by the third generation. North Carolina Furniture (formerly Imperial), an affiliate of Thonet, opened in 1939, as did Carolina Parlor Furniture, which became Gilliam Furniture (later Thomasville Furniture Industries).

After World War II, the South in general came closer to mainstream prosperity and many tenants and sharecroppers left rural areas for jobs in industry. The war had created jobs and added to urban populations while increasing rural incomes with modernized farm machinery, but farms still decreased in numbers and land was taken out of production. There was a tremendous surge in local industry after the war, with larger industries moving in and merging with smaller local businesses.

Schools

It is claimed that they [public graded schools] *furnish the cheapest and best education to be had up to the point to which they go; that they attract a desirable population for a town; that they increase the value of property; and that they, in every way, are helpful to a community...Statesville would do well to give this system of education a trial.*

—J.P. Caldwell, 1883 Landmark

School system development in Iredell can be divided into three periods. The first period, called "Aycock Schools," 1910–1920s, was named in honor of then Governor Aycock. These schools were two- or three-room schools that replaced the typical one-room schoolhouse. The Feimster School was an Aycock school. In 1926, the Bunch family made their home in the old Feimster School, circa 1895, which had opened on North Center Street. The Feimster School was purchased by Fred Bunch Sr. in 1915 and the school became known as the "Bunch House." The distinctive Neoclassical Revival home—with brick veneer, columns and porches added by the Bunch family—remained in the family and now sits amid the residential development of Magnolia Glen. Mulberry Street School was the first graded school in Statesville, and in 1907, public high schools were available for basic studies. In the county, Harmony Academy had such vitality that it became the first official county high school in 1907.

The second period in school development is called "Consolidation," 1920–1930s, when six or seven high schools were created, each with its own elementary school. The first use of buses for student transportation began during this period. Harmony High School had eleven grades, even before Statesville. Troutman had ten grades and Scotts had nine grades. Iredell County had three public school systems: Iredell County Schools, Statesville Graded Schools and Mooresville Graded Schools. Twelve grades only became the norm in the 1940s. The third period is the "High School Consolidation" of the 1960s, which created four large high schools: North, South, East and West Iredell, each with over one thousand students.

Schools for African Americans developed slowly. A bifurcated system was in place with separate schools for the two races. Billingsley Academy, founded by Reverend

Amos Billingsley, grew from a few grades into an accredited high school, Morningside. Mary Charleton Holiday and two charitable organizations were primarily responsible for creating better schools for African Americans. Holiday was the Jeannes Supervisor of Black Schools in Iredell from 1915 until her retirement in 1956. A bas-relief of Ms. Holiday was commissioned from the renowned artist Selma Burke in 1945. It is now in the James Iredell Room, the local history department of the Iredell County Library. See *Heritage of Iredell County*, Vol. I, for more information.

Anna T. Jeannes, a Quaker from Philadelphia, left her estate to provide for black schools; the Rosenwald Fund was dedicated by the president of Sears for the building of schools for African Americans. The Rosenwald schools were the counterpart of the Aycock schools, and these two funds facilitated the consolidation of thirty-nine subpar one-room schools into eleven new community schools. The first new school built was Unity High School in the Belmont area. It was the largest high school in the county by 1960 (it is now an annex for the offices of Iredell–Statesville Schools and a part of the building is set aside to be dedicated to the history of Unity).

The Mooresville Graded School District began in 1905; in 1910, the first class graduated from Mooresville High School. North School Elementary opened in 1912–1913 on the site of an old academy. A school for African Americans was situated near the railroad junction; until the 1920s, that school and the North School were the only two schools in Mooresville. In the late 1930s, a new African American school was built, Dunbar, and later renamed N.F. Woods. The old Central High School, circa 1940s, on

The Mulberry Street School, Statesville, one of the first graded schools established in the town. *Courtesy of the author.*

Moore and Academy Streets, moved to Center Avenue. It eventually became a junior high school. Central was abandoned in 1960 and was later demolished. (Much later, Mitchell College opened a Mooresville campus on the site of the old Central School in the remaining gymnasium building.)

Mitchell College was modernized by President John Scott in the early years of the new century. The physical plant was expanded and it was recognized as a degree-granting institution. Shearer Hall was built in 1907 and the final name change to Mitchell was made in 1917. Mitchell acquired status as a junior college in the early 1920s and became coeducational in 1932.

The Genealogical Society of Iredell County has published the 1917 "Report on Public Schools" in *Iredell County Tracks*; the series, compiled by Mike Trivette, begins in the Fall 2000 issue. There are also articles on school development in *Heritage of Iredell County*, Vol. II.

Mitchell Community College, established in 1854. *Photograph by Max Tharpe. Courtesy of Mitchell Community College.*

Mooresville

Mooresville is coming!

—1889 Landmark

In the twentieth century, Mooresville focused on dry goods, hotels, banks, livery stables, the newspaper, the sawmill and the flour mill. The Midlands Railroad arrived in 1900 and a 1906 bond election facilitated an electric power system that was later purchased by Duke Power. It was noted, however, in *Mooresville, The Early Years*, by W.J. Haselden, that the 1908 silent movies with their mechanical pianos caused the lights to dim all over town! The 1898 phone poles and wires put up by Southern Bell were initially used by Sam Brawley, who operated the first telephone system in 1899, but the Telephone Exchange opened in 1900 and bought his system. The exchange and the operators on the switchboard were located on the second floor of the 1894 Johnson Building. The operators were known as the "hello girls" and both remained at this location until 1951 and the advent of rotary dialing. The building is much the same and now houses the Johnson Square Market Place.

Mooresville Telephone "hello girls" on the second floor of the Johnson Building. *Courtesy of the Mooresville Historical Society.*

The 1894 Johnson Building in Mooresville is today the Johnson Square Market Place. *Courtesy of the author.*

The inimitable D.E. Turner Hardware Store was well established on Main Street by this time, the Central Hotel and the Commercial Hotel were both open north of the depot and the White Oak Roller Mill was always busy. By 1914, the population was over four thousand. There were nine wells for water, four cotton mills, two flour mills, two cottonseed oil mills, a furniture factory, a lumber plant, vehicle shops, bottling works, an ice factory, a mattress factory, sixteen school teachers and eight passenger trains daily. (The original depot was destroyed by fire and the new depot was built in the 1920s.)

Mooresville's oldest bank and the first bank with a state charter, the Bank of Mooresville, circa 1900, became a national bank in 1909 and then Carolina First National Bank after a 1970 merger. The second bank, the Merchants and Farmers Bank, opened in 1908, but was bankrupt by 1932. Piedmont Bank opened at the former location of the Merchants and Farmers Bank in 1946. The bank's unique corner building is now commercial space.

The Mooresville Cooperative Creamery was a joint endeavor by south Iredell dairy farmers who joined forces to establish a creamery in 1914. The Mooresville Ice Cream Company was founded by the Millsaps family, and today the ice cream company and Deluxe continue in its original row of buildings on Broad Street. In 1924, the Mooresville Ice Cream Company developed the original recipe for Deluxe Ice Cream with the help of Charles Mack and Sons, whose confectionary was the inspiration for the recipe for Deluxe Ice Cream, which still proves to be magically irresistible.

The arched entrance of the Bank of Mooresville building (circa 1900). *Courtesy of the author.*

The Mooresville Merchants and Farmers Bank, circa 1908. *Courtesy of the Mooresville Historical Society.*

The former Merchants and Farmers Bank building in Mooresville. The unique corner building is now a commercial site. *Courtesy of the author.*

The Mooresville Ice Cream Co. on Broad Street, home of the 1924 "recipe" for Deluxe Ice Cream. *Courtesy of the author.*

The Mooresville Fire Department organized in 1910 with twelve volunteers using hand reels and leather buckets. In 1914, they bought a hose, wagon and a horse. In 1950, the fire department had three paid and twenty-five volunteer firemen, with a 1921 LaFrance engine. (It would be 1953 before the rescue squad was organized.)

In 1925, Samuel A. Lowrance gave what had been his home on West Center Avenue for use as a hospital. After a small addition was built, the hospital opened in 1926. By 1929, a new four-story hospital was built at Eastern Heights on Statesville and Carpenter Avenues, opening in 1930. In 1939, Lowrance Hospital added Furchess Hall as a school for nurses, and a new wing was built in 1954. Abandoned until a decade ago, the imposing renovation of the expanded former hospital is now used for county offices, the courts and the sheriff's office.

Mooresville, declining to join the library merger of the Iredell County and Statesville Libraries, established its own new library on the site of the former James Elbert Sherrill home. The building is 1939 Georgian Revival, and called "the handsomest small library in North Carolina" by state officials. The bewildering chess game of library moves to get to this new building is astonishing. In 1899, the library began in the living rooms of the Misses Stirewalt and Grierson then was moved to a small office previously used by Dr. McCorkle. Afterward, the library was relocated to the Central Hotel, later moving upstairs over Goodman Drug at Main and Center Streets, before being relegated to

The 1939 Mooresville Public Library is greatly expanded today but retains its Georgian Revival façade. *Courtesy of the Mooresville Historical Society.*

storage at Central High School. The library reopened over the old Mooresville Theater then moved above the Mooresville Drug Store; finally, Miss Lutelle Sherrill Williams built a library on the site of the Sherrill homeplace and donated it to the town in 1939. In 1964, a children's wing was added.

The Mooresville Graded School District administrative offices are housed in a 1937 building on Main Street that was the first federally owned building in the town, constructed by the U.S. Treasury Department as a WPA project for use as a post office. In 1938, Alicia Weincek created a mural for the building depicting the local cotton industry. It can still be seen today on the canvas-covered walls.

Tom McKnight—editor of the *Rounder*, a free handbill circa 1932—rejuvenated the slogan "Queen of Iredell" to describe Mooresville; in *The Inventory of Historic Architecture*, it is stated that Mooresville's downtown has "many original storefronts surviving on a well preserved Main Street." The present depot was built around 1924–1925, and by that time, the main business district of town, the central depot and its surrounding buildings on four corners, had the form that it has today with Victorian buildings in the Romanesque, Italianate Revival and Queen Anne styles. The northwest corner storefronts are said to be "the most perfectly preserved streetscape in the entire district."

After the Depression, Mooresville had three lumber mills, farmers' warehousing, oil mills, shops and businesses, the largest creamery in the area, an ironworks, a flour mill, a cotton mill employing two thousand people, twelve churches, one hospital and fire and police departments. William L. Brown relates in *Around These*

The 1937 Mooresville Post Office on Main Street is now home to the Mooresville Graded School District administrative offices. *Courtesy of the author.*

View of North Main Street, Mooresville. *Courtesy of the author.*

Tracks a description of Mooresville in the 1930s and 1940s as having irreplaceable and sometimes irrepressible charm. Main Street was said to be busy on a Saturday, with shoppers and patrons of the three movie theaters. "Every parking place was filled on Main and Broad!" Men played checkers at the corner grocery, mountain peddlers went door to door selling apples and the woods beyond the wagon path that was later Broad Street were called the "gambling woods" because of the illicit games conducted there.

Statesville

The resources are here, the spirit is here, the opportunity is here, and the time is here!
—from "Attractive Statesville," a 1910 Commercial Club Publication

During the 1920s, development in towns increased opportunities for professional business people and a growing middle class of white-collar workers. The resulting social change, industrial growth, road improvements and school consolidation created big changes in the sleepy little towns. It was the electric age with indoor plumbing, refrigeration, telephones and automobiles all being commonplace in the first third of the century and widespread after World War II. The old country skills of spinning, weaving, shoemaking and carriage building became curiosities, eventually falling into the category of arts and crafts, but mostly gone like the once numerous covered bridges in the county.

The Statesville Chamber of Commerce that had begun in 1889 was taken over by the Commercial Club in 1910. The new organization in 1920 became a tax-supported chamber by 1925 and it was chartered by the state in 1927. In 1921, the Statesville Rotary became a member of Rotary International and was the first civic club in Statesville.

The Billingsley Hospital—opened in 1900 and having last been used during the flu epidemic of 1916–1918—was closed early in the twentieth century. In January of 1920, the thirty-five-bed Carpenter-Davis Hospital was opened at Sharpe and Center Streets by F.A. Carpenter and James W. Davis. In 1923, a school for nurses, begun at Billingsley, was opened at Long's Hospital. By 1925, Davis Hospital had been built on West End Avenue. The new fifty-bed hospital had a nurse-training school as well as a blood bank. A 1952 addition expanded the hospital to two hundred beds. The hospital is now relocated as Davis Regional Medical Center and the old hospital building is the home of Wilson Security Services. See *Heritage of Iredell County*, Vol. I, for more information.

Independent creameries had operated since 1900 but Carnation, opening their condensery on West Front Street, offered a year-round venue for dairy farmers. The sprawling white building still stands on the site and Panther Plastics operates there. Carnation, whose 1938 establishment of the creamery provided the impetus for an increase in dairy farms, caused dairying to skyrocket and made the state first in dairy products in the nation. Superior Dairies, an independent home-owned and -operated dairy, opened in 1941 in a unique art deco building at 1151 West Front Street. Sealtest joined the mid-century dairy business buying Iredell milk. The county was the largest producer of grade A milk in the state.

Eventually beef and poultry rose to compete with dairy in Iredell. By mid-century, the county had over 375,000 acres in crops, livestock, hay and grain. Small grains such as wheat and oats, and row crops such as cotton and tobacco, remained important, but cotton gradually lost its market share. North Iredell's 23,000 acres of cotton progressively diminished to hundreds of acres after the Depression.

The banking industry naturally felt the impact of the Depression and there were many closures. The First National Bank fell victim to the crashing economy, as well as the second town bank, Statesville Loan and Trust. The Statesville Merchants and Farmers Bank, the third to open in 1908, became NCNB, then later, the Bank of America. The 1909 Commercial National Bank (the Industrial Bank circa 1925), located at Court and Center Streets, was in an imposing 1907 building with massive granite columns that were then the largest solid granite columns in the state. The bank became the Bank of Statesville and moved to the old First National Bank building on the square in 1937. Its former site, at Court and Center Streets, is now Kenneth Wooten and Associates. The Bank of Statesville later merged with BB&T. For details on the Rubik's Cube of local bank failures, mergers, name changes and acquisitions, see Homer Keever's *Iredell, Piedmont County*.

In 1931, Statesville Printing began a semiweekly, the *Statesville Record*; in 1951, the *Record* and the *Landmark* merged. The Iredell County Library has microfilm copies of the *Landmark* from its inception, and a digital photo album of early Statesville and Iredell with several hundred photos from the North Carolina State Archives. The *Record and Landmark* office has a number of pre–Civil War issues of the *Iredell Express* on microfilm, as well as random issues of the more temporary publications, and copies of the *Landmark* from 1874.

Public libraries grew from the early subscription libraries and in 1917, the Statesville Board of Aldermen called for the first public library system. The Women's Club completed the plans by 1921. The first library was a small brick building on East Broad Street with a collection from private donors. The second library was on the second floor of a building at North Center and West Broad Streets. The third library was a room at city hall, circa 1931, with a full-time librarian. (Statesville and Mooresville worked together at this time and donated books for the first bookmobile.) The fourth library, circa 1939, was a Works Project building on West Broad Street near the college. Still standing, it is now a school. In 1967, Statesville Public Library and the Iredell County Library, which had been located in the old Long's Hospital, merged. Water Street became the new library site in 1976, and now Tradd Street is the home of the newest iteration of the Iredell County Library.

The Statesville Merchants and Farmers Bank. *Courtesy of the Statesville Historical Collection of Dr. Steve Hill.*

The present town clock, or "the clock tower," as the building is commonly called by Statesville residents. *Courtesy of the author.*

The 1909 Commercial National Bank in Statesville. *Courtesy of the author.*

The 1939 Statesville Public Library on West Broad Street. *Courtesy of the author.*

Mid-Century

Our wisdom we prefer to think, is of our own gathering, while, if the truth be told, it is, most of it,
the last coin of a legacy that dwindles with time.

—Evelyn Waugh, Brideshead Revisited

Mid-century Statesville had grown to nearly six thousand acres with a population of seventeen thousand, and the quietly prosperous and contented 1950s proved to be a vibrant time for the arts in Statesville and greater Iredell County. Iredell Museums was founded at the old pump station on Museum Road, then Pump Station Road, in 1956. The town's first municipal water and sewer system dated from 1899 at the pumping station. This plant closed in the early 1950s when a new plant was built near Turnersburg. After fifty-two years of industrial use, the pump station was rented to a group of citizens with a dream of having a county museum. The Arts and Science Museum was born and prospered on the site for fifty more years before it was renamed the Iredell Museum of Arts and Heritage, and later merged with the Children's Museum of Iredell County to form Iredell Museums in 2003. The old pump station is now a learning center and the nearby museum Farmstead is a popular site for special backcountry events, reenactments and demonstrations. A downtown gallery hosts art exhibits and a children's site at the Signal Hill Mall provides education and entertainment for younger citizens. The thirty-three naturalized acres on Museum Road feature walking trails, with woodland, creek and bog.

The 1899 water-pumping station in Statesville. Later the Arts and Science Museum. *Courtesy of Iredell Museums.*

On another note, the MacDowell Music Club celebrated its centennial in 2007. The club had arisen from the 1907 merger of the old North Carolina State Orchestra and the Apollo Club; by 1917, it was one of the six charter members of the North Carolina Federation of Music Clubs. It is still a vibrant organization today, encouraging music students and offering scholarships. The Iredell Concert Association was formed in 1947 when community concerts began in Statesville and, joining with the North Carolina Symphony Society in Mooresville in 1981, the Iredell Concert Association as we know it today was formed. The Lake Norman Orchestra and the Festival of Music also provide terpsichorean entertainments locally. The Old Time Fiddler's Convention in Union Grove began in 1924 as a fundraiser for Union Grove High School through the efforts and imagination of H.P. Van Hoy, and was continued by his sons, Harper and Pierce Van Hoy. In the 1970s, Harper Van Hoy established the Old Time Fiddler's and Bluegrass Festival at Fiddler's Grove in Union Grove. It was designated as a "Local Legacy" in 2000, as part of the Library of Congress Bicentennial. The third generation of the Van Hoy family now operates the festival organization and continues this "living museum" of traditional music.

It has been said, "There's something in the water in Iredell County, that it creates so many artists!" Well-known local artists include MacKendree Long, a minister and much-collected "outsider artist," and his grandson, Ben Long, the fresco artist who created the Statesville Civic Center fresco as well as others in the state. Robert

Steele, from Statesville, is a nationally renowned painter. Max Tharpe, revered local photographer who documented mid-century life, has donated his extensive collection of prints to Mitchell College, including his 1951 *Juicy Fruit Smile*, which was adopted by the apple industry as their logo. Dr. Selma Burke, an internationally known sculptor from Mooresville, is known as a Harlem Renaissance artist (she sculptured the likeness of President Franklin D. Roosevelt, unveiled after his death, and that image is also used on the face of the dime). Dr. Burke's portrait and her bust of Dr. Davies McLelland are on display in the Mooresville Public Library. In 1990, Dr. Burke exhibited twelve sculptures at the location of the old Arts and Science Museum. The Artists' Guild of Statesville operates a gallery in the Signal Hill Mall. The Mooresville Artists' Guild, established in 1966, took up residence in the old AT&O train depot on Main Street in 1978, which now flourishes as the Depot Visual Arts Center. A new art guild has been established for Lake Norman artists as well. (This list is brief because lack of space does not permit the naming of all of the working artists, past and present, in this county.) Suffice it to say, indeed there must be something in the water!

The opening of a number of manufacturing concerns and industries brought middle-class prosperity to a large segment of the population in Statesville. Whereas Mooresville's development was stalled in the 1950s, in the 1960s, a plan by Duke Power resulted in the most spectacular development in Iredell County and a boost for Mooresville that has literally recreated the town. The 1962 Cowan's Ford Dam Project resulted in the formation of Lake Norman, an enormous man-made lake named for Norman Cocke, president of Duke Energy at that time. The largest man-made body of water in the state, it is sometimes called an inland sea, with over five hundred miles of shoreline. Both the lake and Duke Power State Park opened in 1965. (The lake covered both the site of a Revolutionary War battle between Cornwallis and local regulars led by General William Davidson, and over thirty thousand acres of family farmland.)

Mooresville's municipal water system originally dated from 1909 and consisted of three wells. In 1923, a pump station was added on Byers Creek. In 1962, a modern filtration plant was built near U.S. 21 that used water from the lake. The formation of the lake provided electric power for the Piedmont and began to revitalize the Mooresville business district, whose Main Street and outlying arteries have been almost literally electrified with growth! The largest town on the lakeshore, Mooresville is now known as the "port city" and is experiencing unprecedented growth. (Mooresville is also sometimes called "race city" because of the large number of NASCAR race teams headquartered there, as well as its proximity to Lowe's Motor Speedway.) South Iredell is changed forever—physically, socially and economically. In 1950, the population of Mooresville was a little over seven thousand. In 2007, Mooresville nearly matches Statesville's population of around twenty-five thousand people and growing.

Mooresville Mills and Cascade Mills remained Mooresville's largest employers until the change from textiles began in earnest in 1990 after NAFTA and the Central America Free Trade Agreement. The Mooresville Mill Village at the old Burlington Mill site is a diverse area with a revitalization committee and community watch group to oversee the preservation of the former mill village workers' enclave whose homes are now called

The *Juicy Fruit Smile* by Max Tharpe became a well-known image, adopted by the apple industry as its logo. Max Tharpe was a fixture in the area, documenting life in Iredell County. Max kept in touch with the young boy throughout the years, though the boy tragically lost his life in the Vietnam War. *Courtesy of Mitchell Community College.*

"quaint." Mooresville no longer has active textile mills. Draymore Manufacturing is the site of a go-kart track, and Burlington Mills is redesigned for an enormous mixed-use development on the southern edge of town. The ambitious plans can be seen at www. mooresvillemills.com. In Statesville, the Black and White Knitting Mill, established in 1978 and known for high-quality cloth, is the only African American–owned small-cloth manufacturer. It is still in business today but textile mills generally are struggling

Office furnishings formerly belonging to Dr. R.M. Rickert Jr., optometrist in Statesville, 1947–2004. *Courtesy of Iredell Museums.*

Office furnishings formerly belonging to Dr. Lonnie M. Little, a family doctor in Statesville from 1924 to 1982. *Courtesy of Iredell Museums.*

Statesville street scene, circa 1950. *Courtesy of Iredell Museums.*

to survive and many are now virtually abandoned. Our towns still bear the traces of many of these long-gone industries. It is a pity that they cannot all be remembered and perhaps used for a new purpose in this new century to halt the abandonment of our towns and central cities.

An outflow of population for the roomy suburbs and a consolidation of schools and businesses resulted in megaschools, megabanks, megastores and even megachurches in meganeighborhoods in parts of the country. Are we inching toward a reversal of this trend? To at least balance the scales, we need to look at our towns, our historic buildings, homes and institutions with an eye toward preserving our heritage and the historical integrity of our surroundings. This will be our legacy.

Chapter 5

The Twenty-First Century

Preserving Our Past to Enhance Our Future

Our Future

What we owe the future is not a new start, for we can only begin with what has happened. We owe the future the past-the long knowledge-that is the potency of time to come.

-Wendell Berry

A professor of urban planning wrote in the November 8, 2007 Statesville *Record and Landmark*, "When we looked at this seven or eight years ago, growth was on the horizon. Now it's here." With a population boom within the next decade guaranteed, the issue of retaining small-town charm and rural beauty is a big issue! Jason Goodwin wrote, "A city (or place) endures, which also grows, forever adding new identities to the old." So the answer lies in the restoration of our past, adding the new to the historic, not just haphazardly replacing the old. A lack of regard for our own history is a fatal flaw and will reveal itself in unexpected ways: a lack of archival materials in our library, a dearth of pertinent exhibits in our county museum, a cookie-cutter faux charm in our new buildings and a loss of historic structures that would anchor our towns as well as inform us. Our historic collections, archives and structures are remarkable resources and breathe life into the present. Nina Stritzler, director of the Bard Graduate Center, wrote, "Negation of the past is an inaccurate perception of how to innovate for the future." Even our innovation is at risk when we neglect our history.

Historic preservation organizations fulfill the need to maintain the unique character of our county by keeping the past safe from careless development, thus retaining the flavor of "bygone days." P.F. Laugenour wrote, "We spend time and talent studying the history of countries and people who lived thousands of miles from us, thousands of years ago, while we are perfectly oblivious to what has occurred right around us and the part our own people played in the performance." We must not remain in this oblivious state; preservation organizations and commissions attempt to ensure that we do not do so. The 1978 *Inventory of Historic Architecture* recorded hundreds of significant sites in Iredell County ranging from the mid-eighteenth century to the early twentieth century.

There are five districts in Statesville listed as historic districts, and many homes and buildings are listed on the National Register. Statesville has four central residential

Early twentieth-century homes on Water Street, Statesville. *Courtesy of the author.*

Former home of J.C. Steele on Mulberry Street, Statesville—the oldest residence in Academy Hill, circa 1900. *Courtesy of the author.*

A 1910 Neoclassical Revival home on North Center Street, Statesville. *Courtesy of the author.*

A 1918 Elizabethan Revival–style home on the corner of Walnut and Mulberry Streets, Statesville. *Courtesy of the author.*

neighborhoods that developed in the nineteenth century. Because of slow development in the mid-twentieth century, many Victorian buildings have survived to give Statesville a unique, irreplaceable atmosphere. The historic districts are Broad Street/Davie Avenue, Mitchell College, Academy Hill, Race Street and the Downtown Commercial District. The oldest buildings in Statesville date from between 1820 and 1860, built on the eve of the Civil War in the Greek Revival style. Others date from the late nineteenth to the early twentieth centuries in Italianate, Romanesque, Gothic and Queen Anne Revival styles. Early twentieth-century styles included Neoclassical Revival, Colonial and Neocolonial Revival. From 1915 to 1925, the Elizabethan Revival and Regency styles were joined by the popular bungalow-style home.

The Historic Properties Commission, formed between 1976 and 1978, governs the historic accuracy of all exterior improvements while encouraging restoration and preservation. President Richard Boyd stated their mission: "To preserve what we have, halt any loss of significant property, and educate the public about historic preservation." Preservation Statesville, a newer organization, promotes historic houses with an annual Christmas Tour of Historic Homes and works toward enhancing public awareness of the necessity of historic preservation. In the 1940 *Landmark*, William Powell, preeminent historian for the state and author of the recently released *Encyclopedia of North Carolina*, listed features that abound on the homes in Statesville, including gables, towers, gingerbread trim, mansard rooflines and multicolored stained-glass windows.

The Mooresville Historic Preservation Commission was established in 2000 and processed the first house to be designated as a local landmark in 2008. The second house to receive that designation from the commission will be the Espy Brawley House. Iredell County adopted two buildings in Mooresville previously—the library and one historic house—and they have now been turned over to the Mooresville Commission, which is in the process of completing an inventory of all of the historic buildings in the town. South Academy Street is probably the oldest district, dating from the 1870s. Later styles on other streets include Italianate Revival, Queen Anne and Neoclassical Revival. The Mooresville Downtown Commission was established in 1988 as a "main street revitalization" organization, whose mission was to stop the decline of Mooresville's downtown. The commission and downtown business owners have worked well together to ensure the survival of the quaint village atmosphere of the town, whose center, the four corners surrounding the depot, is remarkably well-preserved.

The identity of Iredell County is changing. Growth is surging northward from the Charlotte metropolitan area and from Mooresville, our "port city" in south Iredell, with her burgeoning lakefront prosperity. Statesville, the "best town in North Carolina" in the nineteenth century, grew into the "city of progress" by the mid-twentieth century and now bears the title "crossroads of the future." It is an apt title. Statesville's crossroads had its beginnings as a part of the Eisenhower Interstate System and Interstates 40 and 77 became the largest highway interchange in North Carolina, making Statesville a literal crossroads.

The population of Iredell County was nearly 150,000 in 2007, and County Manager Joel Mashburn now expects the population to reach 175,000 within the next few years.

A Dutch Colonial Revival home derived from the eighteenth-century styles in New York. West End Avenue, Statesville. *Courtesy of the author.*

Victorian styling on Walnut Street, Statesville. *Courtesy of the author.*

Academy Street, Mooresville. *Courtesy of the author.*

The former Espy Brawley house, Mooresville. *Courtesy of the author.*

County Tax Administrator Bill Doolittle wrote in the 2007 *Record and Landmark*, "People move in for the lake, the good weather, and a lower cost of living." And it is true that the county has all of those attributes, as well as diverse mineral deposits, benign climate, soil where almost any crop can be grown, a variety of natural stone and clay and unspoiled rural expanses and farmland.

Our agricultural heritage, begun in the eighteenth century, now includes nearly 1,300 farms with 147,000 total acres in 2002, according to Joel Reese, local history librarian at the Iredell County Library. Most of these farms are family owned with an average size of 116 acres. An "agricultural district" now exists in Iredell, covering over 13,000 acres and 86 farms. An Enhanced Voluntary Agricultural District bill was passed by the North Carolina General Assembly in 2005; if passed locally, Iredell will be the sixth county in the state to establish the enhanced districts.

In 2007, Ken Vaughn wrote in the *Record and Landmark* that Iredell was the leading dairy county in North Carolina, with fifty-three dairy farms producing twenty-eight million gallons of milk annually from approximately twelve thousand cows. Almost half of this milk is produced at farms with fewer than two hundred cows. "Got milk? Yes, we've got milk, and bucolic rural areas, and an enormous lake, and charming small towns, as well as over two hundred years of history!"

The "Walking Tour of Statesville," with audio information available at the depot and at the Iredell County Library on Tradd Street, covers thirty-one historic locations. A "Walking Tour of Mooresville" is available at the Mooresville Public Library on South Main Street and is occasionally led by a guide. For a regular taste of the area's history,

An early Statesville Chamber of Commerce photograph. *Courtesy of the Greater Statesville Chamber of Commerce.*

the appetite can be satisfied with bites of information in Bill Moose's regular columns, "Out of Our Past," in the *Record and Landmark* and in O.C. Stonestreet's Sunday column featuring historical subjects for those with an appetite for more. Stonestreet and Cynthia Jacobs also write columns for the *Mooresville Tribune*. Gene Krider, the curator of our local memories of people and places and receiver of information on all things architectural, writes a weekly column in the *Record and Landmark*; Joel Reese also contributes a column to the *Record and Landmark* on history and research.

The Iredell County Library is a remarkable resource in itself. The James Iredell Room has over six thousand books and journals in the local history collection and over three thousand reels in the microfilm collection of records. Included are records of census, industry, agriculture, manufacturing and social statistics. The newspapers on microfilm, including the *Record and Landmark*, are in a continuous run from 1874, with a few issues of the *Iredell Express* (circa 1858), two issues of the *Gazette*, a few copies of the *Mooresville Monitor* from 1885, some copies of the weekly *Register* from the 1890s, the *Mooresville Enterprise* from 1904 to 1947 and the *Mooresville Tribune* from 1940 to the present. The library also has over six hundred individual family histories and city directories from 1907 in Statesville and 1939 in Mooresville. Records can also be found for vital statistics, cemeteries, church and court records, obituaries, school and land records, maps, military service records and estate documents.

The former Charles Mack Warehouse and now the home of the Mooresville Museum. *Courtesy of the author.*

"Save the Depot" poster, designed by Robert Steele, featuring the Statesville Depot that was moved in the 1990s for purposes of preservation. *Courtesy of Iredell Museums.*

The Statesville Depot, after its move "across the tracks." *Courtesy of the author.*

Red clay soil is a dominant feature of the county, and there are still many "red roads" throughout the countryside, sometimes splashed with irresistible red puddles and sometimes hard and dry. Follow the brick-red roads. Explore Iredell. *Photograph by Max Tharpe. Courtesy of Mitchell Community College.*

The newly formed Mooresville Museum was established in 2005. For more information, see www.themooresvillemuseum.org. The long-established Iredell Museums, circa 1956, is now searching for a new home in downtown Statesville in which to display its local collections. For more information, see www.iredellmuseums.org. The Genealogical Society of Iredell County works tirelessly to archive and to publish historical papers as well as to publish a quarterly review. See selected excerpts in *Iredell County Tracks*.

Our forebears left an incomparable legacy and we have a wonderful county. Let us keep it that way, for ourselves and for our descendants! It is a gift that only we can give. Zachary Karabell said, "History matters. It is up to each of us to use it well."

Sources

Blythe, Legette. *James W. Davis.* Charlotte, NC: William Loftin Publishing, 1956.

Brown, Louis. "Pre-History of Iredell County." In *Iredell County Landmarks.* Edited by the Publication Committee, Elizabeth Stimson, Chair. Statesville, NC: Iredell County American Revolution Bicentennial Commission, 1976.

Brown, William L. *Around These Tracks.* Gastonia, NC: Brown, 1993.

Campbell, Joseph. *The Power of Myth.* New York: Doubleday, 1988.

Chambers, Captain H.A. "The Confederacy." *The Landmark,* 1913.

Debelius, Maggie. "The European Challenge." Edited by Time-Life Books, Thomas Flaherty, Editor-in-Chief. Richmond, VA: Time-Life Books, 1992.

Erdoes, Richard, and Alfonso Ortiz. *American Indian Myths and Legends.* New York: Pantheon, 1984.

Evans, Virginia Fraser. *Iredell County Landmarks.* Edited by the Publication Committee, Elizabeth Stimson, Chair. Statesville, NC: Iredell County American Revolution Bicentennial Commission, 1976.

Fries, Adelaide L., ed. *Records of the Moravians in North Carolina,* Vol. I. North Carolina State Archives. Raleigh, NC: Edwards and Broughton Print Co., 1922-2006.

Frye, Juanita. *Looking Back: A Pictorial History of Statesville and Iredell County.* Edited by the Statesville *Record and Landmark.* Statesville, NC: *Record and Landmark,* 1998.

Haire, John. "Commanding Presence." *Our State Magazine,* October, 2007.

SOURCES

Haselden, W.J. *Mooresville, the Early Years.* Mooresville, NC: Mooresville Chamber of Commerce, 1973.

Herring, Mac. "Mooresville History in Your Pocket." The Mooresville Museum. http://www.themooresvillemuseum.org/history/hist_writ.htm.

Herring, Ralph M. "Memories of Mac." The Mooresville Museum. http://www.themooresvillemuseum.org/history/hist_writ.htm.

Jacobs, Cindy. *Images of America–Mooresville.* Charleston, SC: Arcadia Publishing, 2007.

Jasanoff, Maya. "Loyal to a Fault." *New York Times Magazine,* July 1, 2007, national edition.

Keever, Homer. *Iredell, Piedmont County.* North Carolina: Iredell County Bicentennial Commission, 1976.

Kellogg, Robert G. "Rowan, Gem of the Piedmont." In *Heritage of Rowan County.* Edited by Katherine Petrucelli. Salisbury, NC: Genealogical Society of Rowan County, Inc., 1991.

Kluger, Richard. *Seizing Destiny.* New York: Random House, 2007.

Laugenour, Philip F. "The Collected Papers of Dr. P.F. Laugenour." In *Iredell County Tracks, Vols. 23-30.* Statesville, NC: Genealogical Society of Iredell County, 2000-2007.

Lawson, John. *A New Voyage to Carolina.* Chapel Hill: University of North Carolina Press, 1984.

Lederer, John. *Discoveries of John Lederer in Three Several Marches from Virginia to the West of Carolina.* Trans. from German by Sir William Talbot. London: Printed by J.C. for S. Heyrick, 1672.

Linn, Jo White. "The Great Philadelphia Wagon Road, a Study of Migrations." In *Heritage of Rowan County.* Edited by Katherine Petrucelli. Salisbury, NC: Genealogical Society of Rowan County, Inc., 1991.

Miller, Mildred, Edith Walker, and Irene Black, eds. *Heritage of Iredell County*, Vol. I. Statesville, NC: Genealogical Society of Iredell County, 1980.

———. *Heritage of Iredell County*, Vol. II. Statesville, NC: Genealogical Society of Iredell County, 2000.

Mooresville Downtown Commission. "A Walking Tour." http://www. downtownmooresville.com.

"Mooresville's Early Town Politics," *The Historical News*, November 2006, Southern Edition, Vols. 26-57NC.

Mooresville Tribune. "A Look Back." 1998. Special Section: History.

Moose, William. *A History of Mitchell Community College.* Statesville, NC: Mitchell Community College, 2005.

Parker, Mattie E. Edwards, William S. Price, Robert J. Cain, eds. *The Colonial Records of North Carolina*, second series, Vols. III and IV. North Carolina State Archives. Raleigh, NC: Carolina Tercentenary Commission, 1963.

Parramore, Thomas. "The North Carolina Illustrated Timeline." In *North Carolina, Reflections of 400 Years*. Edited by Epley and Associates. Raleigh, NC: Branch Bank and Trust Company, 1984.

Ramsey, R.W. *Carolina Cradle.* Chapel Hill: University of North Carolina Press, 1964.

Rights, Douglas. *The American Indian in North Carolina.* Winston-Salem, NC: John F. Blair Publishing, 1957.

Rockwell, E.F. "Manners and Customs in the Old Times." *Carolina Watchman,* 1847.

Royce, Charles, and James Mooney. *The Cherokee.* Chicago: Aldine Publishing, 1975.

Statesville Record and Landmark. "Bicentennial Edition." 1988. Special Section: Commemorative.

Statesville Record and Landmark. "Centennial Edition." 1974. Special Section: Anniversary.

Statesville Record and Landmark. "Fort Dobbs." 1970. Special Section: History.

Statesville Record and Landmark. "Past and Present." 1961. Special Section: History.

Statesville Record and Landmark. "Pictorial Edition." 1955. Special Section.

Statesville Record and Landmark. "Rotary Progress and History Edition." 1961. Special Section: Progress.

Statesville Record and Landmark and Mooresville Tribune. "Discover Iredell." 2007. Special

SOURCES

Section: Local History.

Stokes, Ruth L., and Gary Freeze. *Inventory of Historic Architecture in Statesville and Iredell County N.C.* Raleigh, NC: Department of Cultural Resources, 1978.

Wall, Steve, and Harvey Arden. *Wisdom Keepers.* Hillsboro, OR: Beyond Words Publishing, 1990.

Wagner, Gail E., and Jamie Civitello. *Ancient Gardening in South Carolina.* South Carolina: University of South Carolina College of Liberal Arts, 2000.

Watt, W.N. *Statesville, My Home Town.* Taylorsville, NC: Watt, 1996.

Weatherford, Jack. *Native Roots.* New York: Crown Publishing, 1991.

Wheeler, John Hill. *Historical Sketches of North Carolina from 1584 to 1851.* Philadelphia: Lippencott, Grambo & Co., 1851.

Zinn, Howard. *A People's History of the United States.* New York: Harper Collins, 1999.